A ⌐⌐⌐⌐⌐⌐⌐

Memory

Lectures in Honour of
Elchanan and Miriam Elkes

A Sacred Memory

Lectures in Honour of Elchanan and Miriam Elkes

Edited by Professor Aubrey Newman
and Barbara Butler

School of Historical Studies, University of Leicester with
Christians Aware

First published in 2003 by the University of Leicester
University Road
Leicester, LE1 7RH.

ISBN: 1 873372 20 5

Cover designed by Paula Curtis

Original painting by Joel Elkes

Contents

Introduction

I am very happy to write a short appreciation on the occasion of the publication of this book in honour of my parents.

I remember the day many years ago when I went to the History Department in the Attenborough Building of the University of Leicester for the first time. I bravely jumped onto the 'paternoster' and when I jumped off again I was cold and dishevelled. I found my way to a small room almost at the top of the building and when I entered I could see nothing but books and papers. I had to look hard to see a face in the middle of it all but I finally did see Professor Aubrey Newman.

I explained that I would like to arrange a lecture in memory of my parents. I told Aubrey a little of the family history and to my amazement he knew some of it through his work as a historian. I was both surprised and delighted when he said that his family was also from Lithuania. I will always be grateful to him for the work we have shared over the years, as lecture has followed lecture. It has been a special pleasure for me to know that the lectures have been occasions for the city of Leicester and the university to share in growing understanding of what our community has endured.

I am also grateful to all the lecturers for their work and contributions towards an understanding of the history of suffering and hope for so many people in the 1930s and 40s. Now I must thank them also, for their contribution towards this book.

Special thanks are due to Aubrey Newman and Barbara Butler for their work, which has made the book a reality. In working with Barbara and

i

with Christians Aware I have discovered a wonderful overlap in both vision and practical work with the work I do in the Elchanan Elkes Foundation. I can't begin to thank my brother Joel, who was one of the lecturers and who has been the one solid presence who has never left me.

I had felt powerless to commemorate my parents until the lectures began. I have never attended a lecture, because the content was always too much to listen to, but I have always arrived just before the end, to meet and thank people.

My father was the physician to Sir Thomas Preston, the British ambassador in Lithuania, who encouraged us all as a family when my brother and myself came to England before the Second World War. Many years later I visited Sir Thomas and Lady Preston and for the first time heard the story of how my mother had arranged a sewing box for Lady Preston to take with her on the hazardous journey when she and her husband had to flee as the German army advanced into Lithuania. She never forgot the kindness of my parents. Their son attended the lectures until his death.

This book, in honour of my parents, is a reminder of their kindness and of the pricelessness of human kindness which is the main tool we all have in combating cruelty and oppression towards any people anywhere in the world.

Sara Elkes

Preface

The Elkhanan and Miriam Elkes Memorial Lecture was established in 1991, and came about at the initial suggestion of Sara Elkes, the daughter of Elchanan and Miriam Elkes. She, encouraged by her brother, Dr Joel Elkes, and in conjunction with the Elchanan Elkes Association for Intercommunity Understanding, established it as a series to be held in the University of Leicester under the auspices of the Stanley Burton Centre for Holocaust Studies. The Centre is indebted to her for this generous decision to establish this lecture in honour of her parents.

The Elkes family; Miriam; Elchanan; Joel and Sara

The lectures are intended to throw light upon various aspects of the Holocaust, and while each lecture stands on its own they make collectively a substantial contribution to an understanding of these events. They cover a period of over ten years, in effect the period of time when Professor Aubrey Newman was the Honorary Director of the Centre. Over the years since the initial lecture of 1991 a number of distinguished scholars have accepted invitations to deliver these lectures, and the sponsors of this publication would wish to pay tribute and express their gratitude to those scholars of international reputation who agreed to participate and for having provided the texts on which this volume is based. It has not been possible to include the texts of the lectures given by Professor John Klier of University College London and by Professor Steven Katz of Boston University but the editors would wish to express the gratitude of the sponsors of the lectures for their having delivered their lectures.

They would also wish to express their gratitude to the School of Historical Studies in the University of Leicester which has very generously made this publication possible and to Christians Aware which has helped to co-sponsor it as a personal tribute to the work of Sara Elkes.

The lectures, with one exception, are published as delivered. The inaugural lecture, by Dr Joel Elkes and in memory of his father, was an emotional and highly charged piece of work and was indeed more (and longer) than would normally be expected from such lectures. Indeed, it was later published as a book in its own right in the United Kingdom and then later, with slight changes, in the United States. The editors are grateful to the American publishers, the Paraclete Press, for their permission to reprint some chapters and thus make possible a more complete record of this series. Clearly, there is a certain amount of duplication and repetition between the lectures, but the editors feel that that should stand without further re-editing.

At one of the lectures a member of the audience divulged that she had been born in the Kovno Ghetto and related the circumstances in which her life had been saved by Dr Elkes' direct actions; she was invited to contribute her testimony to this volume as a further tribute to his memory.

In the earlier publication Professor Newman wrote a preface which is included here as an attempt to set into context both the series and the significance of Dr Elchanan Elkes himself.

Leadership in the Kovno Ghetto

In the pattern of Jewish life in Eastern Europe before 1939 an important part was played by the Jewish Councils and by individuals who played an important part in the leadership of their communities. However with the coming of the war and the consequent disruption of all life in Poland, Jewish and non-Jewish alike, many of these leaders disappeared and the communities were left floundering. At the same time however the new German administration decreed that the Jewish population should be concentrated into a number of ghettos, each administered by a Nazi appointed Judenrat and each headed by a Jewish Elder. The decrees which established these institutions made it clear that the individuals who made them up had no option but to accept the office which was imposed upon them and that they were personally and collectively 'fully responsible' to the Nazi authorities for the 'exact and punctual execution' of all orders delivered to them. The leaders who were brought forward through these decrees were often enough not the 'natural leaders' of the community. Indeed, in many cases the Germans when faced with leaders nominated by the Jewish communities shot the first nominees and 'invited' the communities to make a further set of choices. In other cases the Germans themselves nominated an individual who was to take over as the head of the Ghetto Council.

Over the next years these councils had the task of organising the daily life of the Jewish populations, of regulating rations, of allocating housing, and in many cases of ensuring the continuance of the hospitals, the orphanages, and all aspects of life. All relations between the German occupying authorities and the Jewish communities had to pass through the hands of these Councils which had in consequence to establish a complete bureaucracy within the ghetto. Each ghetto was fully enclosed and within the ghetto there was established a police force responsible for maintaining law and order as well as implementing the decrees of the Council.

As a consequence there has been a considerable argument amongst historians about the part played by such men as Jacob Gens of Vilna, of Adam Czerniakow of Warsaw, or of Chaim Rumkowski of Lodz. Some writers have maintained that without their willingness to obey German orders, however reluctant such acquiescence might have been, it would not have been possible for the Germans to have implemented the 'Final Solution'. Others have pointed to the ways in which such leaders did their best to establish some order for the populations placed under their guidance, and that their aim was to try and preserve as many as possible in the hope that eventually some would survive the war and continue a pattern of Jewish life. Over the past few years, as a result of the work of historians such as Israel Trunk, Israel Guttman, and Yehuda Bauer, a great deal of light has been thrown upon the agonies faced by these leaders.

There was however one important difference between the ghettos of that part of Poland occupied by the Germans in 1939 and those which came under German control after June 1941. The full horrors of German occupation had not developed immediately in Poland, but the ghettos further east, and above all in Lithuania, were established only after the initial waves of massacres conducted by the local populations, but instigated by the German armies and Einsatzgruppen immediately after the German invasions. The Jewish leadership could have had no illusions about what was to happen to them, while those members of the Jewish communities who had survived the first wave of massacres were also only too aware of what had been happening around them.

It is in this atmosphere that the Jews of Kovno were instructed to appoint a leader and it is under these circumstances that Elchanan Elkes eventually allowed his name to go forward. Avraham Tory's Diary shows very clearly the debates that took place and the procedures as a result of which Dr Elkes received a vote of confidence from his leading contemporaries. It was to be this fact however which marked him out amongst the leaders of the Ghettos of eastern Europe. He had not sought office, but rather was it forced upon him. On the other hand it was not forced upon him by the occupying forces, but rather by the Jews themselves. There can be no clearer statement of Elkes' unique position than that made by an eminent Rabbi of the Community:

> How terrible is our position that we are not offering the revered Dr Elkes the respected position of Head of the Jewish Community of Kovno but the shameful and humiliating one of 'Head of the Jews', who is to represent us before the Germans. But please understand, dear and beloved Dr Elkes, that only to the Nazi murderers will you be 'Head of the Jews'. In our eyes you will be the head of our community, elected in our most tragic hour, when blood runs from all of us and the murderer's sword is suspended over our heads. It has fallen to your part to accept duties of unequalled difficulty, but at the same time it is also a great privilege and a deed of charity, and you do not have the right to escape from it; stand at our head, defend us, you shall be with us and we will be with you until we arrive at the great day of salvation.

If that was the way in which he was appointed the representative leader of the Jews of Kovno, the works of Avraham Tory and of William Mishell illustrate very clearly the ways in which he fulfilled the responsibilities laid upon him. Over and over again they show the ways in which, at very real danger to his own life, he maintained his principles and did his best to defend his community. And he had *always the moral advantage that, compared with the others in similar positions, he had no personal ambitions. They illustrate clearly his moral ascendancy.*

Those who have to teach the history of Eastern Europe in these years have always had the responsibility of trying to understand what led the Jewish leaders to act as they did. At the same time it has always been important that we have had the example of Elchanan Elkes to set beside the others.

It was fitting that the initial lecture was delivered by Professor Joel Elkes as a personal tribute. All who were present on that occasion were aware of the personal strain and emotion which this lecture represented for both of them. But it was a fitting tribute to a man who all feel had accepted an awesome challenge and met it bravely, who at the time when the ghetto was destroyed emerged untarnished, having preserved the lives of a significant number of its inhabitants.

The Stanley Burton Centre for Holocaust Studies was founded in 1990, and was refounded under its present name in 1993 under the auspices of the Burton Trusts. It is a non-profit teaching and research centre within the University of Leicester, and is dedicated to the extension of knowledge about the Holocaust to the widest possible range of the academic and general public.

Christians Aware is an international and educational charity which works to offer opportunities and resources for encounter between people of different backgrounds experiences and faiths towards possibilities of reconciliation in times of trouble and development and peace work. In Leicester it has been working closely for a number of years with Sara Elkes and the Elchanan Elkes Association for International Understanding

Values, Belief and Survival: Dr Elchanan Elkes and the Kovno ghetto

Joel Elkes

Introduction

When my sister, Sara Elkes, the founder of this lecture, suggested that I deliver the lecture on which this Memoir is based, I acceded at once. Yet, within hours, the full implications of this brotherly impulse surfaced in their stark truth. It is not easy, in any circumstances, to speak in public of one's parents. The hidden treasures of youth are private, and, to retain their magic, of necessity, must remain private. The public events which have made Dr Elkes a major figure in the history of the Holocaust were events at which I was not present. I was therefore at a double disadvantage. A loyal son is not the best of witnesses, and, in any event, I am only a witness once removed. There is also the inner silence which the mind observes in the face of the unthinkable and unspeakable. In my own case my moratorium with myself lasted for more than two decades. In this respect I find I am not alone. The authors I quote worked through a similar predicament.

Yet despite the above reservations I am glad of the opportunity. For my purpose is to connect the person I knew and remember with the person I have learned to know from the accounts of others, and to relate this person to the life, death and destiny of the community which he served and led.

There are, as noted, six persons who occupy a central place in the story I am about to tell. They are my parents, Elchanan and Miriam Elkes, Lucy Elstein-Lavon, Esther Lurie, and Avraham and Pnina Tory.

Elchanan and Miriam Elkes

My father Elchanan Elkes was born in 1879 in Kalvarija, a little township some 35 miles from Kovno, Lithuania. He was the second of six children. His father kept a small general store where my grandfather, Israel Meir Elkes, would move among the barrels and boxes and bags of flour, sugar and cattlefeed, serving his peasant customers with exquisite good manners and humour. In the back of the store was his small study, to which he would retire to dwell on his beloved Talmud. And here – so the story goes – there could at times be seen a handsome red-headed boy reading the encyclopedia in Russian. It is reported that young Elchanan started with the letter A and simply went on. Nobody knows which high school he attended. He graduated from the University of Koenigsberg, across the border from Lithuania, in East Prussia, with distinction in Medicine, in 1903.

The outbreak of World War I saw him a medical officer in the Russian army, moving with his regiment from the Oder to the Urals and back again. He weathered the Russian Revolution in the small town of Orsha. Even then his house provided shelter to White Russians and commissars alike. In 1919 or 1920 he returned to the country of his birth, settling in Kovno (Kaunas), the temporary capital of the newly declared independent Lithuanian Republic. There he established his practice as an internist. It grew and grew. Very rapidly he became the leading physician of the land, counting the President, the Prime Minister and the Diplomatic Corps among his patients. With Dr Berman and Dr Brauns he built the Division of Internal Medicine in the newly founded Jewish Hospital. With Dr Moshe Schwabe – later Rector of the Hebrew University in Jerusalem – and a few others, he established a secondary school – the Hebrew Gymnasium, *Gymnassion Ivry Kovno*, a school in which all subjects were taught in Hebrew, and which later trained some of the brightest future educators and leaders in Israel. Yet he kept away from committees and councils. To the core he was, and remained, a private person.

As I write, I recall his clean features and his smile. His movements were small and graceful. He rarely raised his voice in public, but when he spoke there was warmth and interest and humour in it, which gave anyone in his presence a sense of closeness and courage. Human frailty – including his own – was to him part of the Almighty's prescription for a good and full life. Only in the presence of bigotry, prejudice, and cruelty would his demeanour change. He would then grow silent, a silence often followed by a statement of such devastating directness as to render his hearer dumbfounded and confused. It was, for example, well known in his Russian regiment that antisemitic remarks in the officers' mess were definitely not worth while in the presence of Dr Elkes. On the other hand, he sometimes used to tell me, with a genuine – almost childlike –

delight, of his discussions on Judaism with the British or German or Russian Ambassador.

He was generous to a fault. His waiting room was always full of patients who could not pay, and so was his ward in the Jewish Hospital. Although easily approachable to these patients, he kept his distance with others. It is reported, for example, that when the wife of the Prime Minister called him on a Saturday to ask to see him, he politely enquired whether it was urgent. Being reassured that it was not, he simply suggested: 'It is my Sabbath. However, I would be very glad to see you tomorrow or on Monday.' In times of crisis, his counsel was sought by wielders of power, yet he took the greatest pains to avoid any public office – even service on the boards of the school and the hospital he helped to found.

On his desk there rested a little tablet carrying an inscription taken from the grave of Emmanuel Kant, who was buried in Koenigsberg. 'Two things', it said (I am translating from memory), 'continue to astonish the mind, the more it dwells upon them. One is the starry sky above me, and the other the moral law within me.' Elchanan Elkes really lived these questions and shared them with his children.

Dr Elkes with his staff in the Kovno Hospital

His wife Miriam, whom he wooed and married while teaching her Hebrew in Koenigsberg, was the daughter of a moderately prosperous grain merchant, Moses Malbin, and his wife Esther. Blessed with warmth,

3

vitality, curiosity, and extraordinarily well read, she assimilated the best of German and French culture, while always drawing on the well-springs of her Jewish heritage. Much was self-taught. Her cheerful temperament complemented my father's sometimes sombre mood. She was his complete confidante and life companion. She was a wonderful mother, a fount of joy, optimism, adventure, sheer lifemanship, and full of sound practical advice. The formidable strength and spiritual reserves of this extraordinary woman did not become apparent until the last years of her life. Countless persons have related to Sara and me how they drew on Mrs Elkes' strength in the Ghetto, in the camp, and beyond.

Lucy Elstein-Lavon

Lucy Elstein, who became the secretary of the Ghetto Kovno Council, was the daughter of a charming couple who kept a fragrant-smelling pharmacy on Main Street in Kovno. Fluent in German, Lithuanian, Russian, Hebrew and Yiddish, working closely with Avraham Tory from the beginning of the establishment of the Ghetto, and later, - at Dr Elkes' and the Council's urging – in the Gestapo office, she proved an extraordinary source of intelligence during some of the most critical times in the Ghetto. It was she who, typing memoranda and orders through fresh carbons (which could subsequently be read), passed on information of value to the Council. She was one of the last people to leave Ghetto Kovno. After a deportation and a terrible imprisonment in Stutthof Concentration Camp – where she was with my mother she came to the then Palestine via Italy. She died in Israel in 1981.

Esther Lurie

Esther Lurie was born in Libau, Latvia and trained as an art student in Brussels. She came to Palestine in 1934, to be recognized rapidly as a widely acclaimed artist and designer, and winning the coveted Dizengoff Award in 1938. As fate would have it, she visited relatives in Kovno in 1939 and was overtaken by events, becoming a captive of the Russians and, later, the German occupation. From the inception of the Ghetto in 1941, she became its 'living witness', its unforgettable graphic chronicler. Her records of the unimaginable - drawn in pen, often within hours of an 'Action' - recall Goya's *Horrors of War*. It is hard to fathom whence she drew the strength to put down what she witnessed. Only some 30 paintings out of around 200

4

of her works survived. They were hidden by Avraham Tory and clandestinely taken out with other documents. Her album, *A Living Witness*, taken together with Mr George Kadushin's formidable photographic records, is one of the most precious archives of the Ghetto in existence. After going through concentration camps in Germany and Poland and being liberated by the Red Army, she returned to Palestine in 1945. She received a second Dizengoff Prize in 1946 and the Zussman Award in 1992 and has exhibited extensively in Israel and abroad. Several documentaries record her work. As she says in one of them 'Never did I think that the skills which I acquired in copying Rembrandt and Durer would be put to such use.'

Avraham and Pnina Tory

Avraham Tory – or Avraham Golub, as he was then known – was born in the Lithuanian village of Lazdijai in 1909. His father had qualified as a rabbi, his mother's family were farmers. He studied at the Hebrew school in Marijampole, in which all subjects (as in my school) were taught in Hebrew.

The Zionist ideal – the return of the Jews to Palestine – was to him, as to many of us at the time, a very practical one. He rose rapidly in the Zionist youth movement and remained one of the most senior members of the Maccabi Sports Association, having literally carried its flag in many countries. He briefly studied Law in the United States and completed his studies in Lithuania in 1933. Because of the restricted admission of Jews into the legal profession, he found himself barred from practice. He clerked for a Lithuanian judge (who had graduated at the same time as him) and later became assistant to Professor Simon Beliatskin, Professor of Civil Law and a famous jurist – one of the few Jews on the faculty in Kovno. During the Russian occupation of Lithuania (between 1940 and 1941) he was employed by the Soviet military construction administration. However, having been dismissed and learning that he was to be deported because of his known Zionist activities, he went into hiding, only to return on June 22nd, 1941, on the eve of the German attack on Lithuania and the Soviet Union. That day, or, to be precise, at midnight of that day, Avraham Tory embarked on the task which ensures him a lasting place in Jewish history. Writing in the home of his sister and brother-in-law, Basja and Benjamin Romanovski, he recorded the awesome events of the day when several hundred Jews were brutally murdered in Kovno and its environs by roaming Lithuanian mobs. From then on he set down his testimony as often as he could, usually within a day or so of events, until the last entry in his diary, some two years and nine months later, on January 9th, 1944. The sparseness, economy and stark detail of his writing only heighten the dimensions of the unfathomable tragedy which he set himself to record. For it is one thing to write a diary - even in a prisoner-of-war camp - it is a totally different matter to keep a record of the day when you do not know whether you will survive into the following day. Yet, day by day, he acted on his iron determination to testify unto future generations.

Documentary materials were added to the diary almost daily and the archives grew very rapidly. A safe place for their storage had to be found. The story of the diary and accompanying documents, their retrieval, their travels through four countries with the Torys or in the trust of friends, is a tale which must be told unabridged to fathom its full depth and meaning. Sir Martin Gilbert records it in his introduction to Tory's book. I can only give you a few facts.

The documents, wrapped in greaseproof paper, were packed into five wooden crates and encased in metal sheeting, welded tight for safekeeping. One of the crates contained Tory's last will and testament. The crates were then buried deep below the concrete foundations of a three-storey building known as Block C. Only three people - Avraham Tory, Pnina Sheinson and Shraga Goldschmidt, who had fashioned the crates, - knew their hiding place.

On November 22nd, 1943, Avraham Tory clandestinely took Pnina Sheinson and her daughter Shulamith out of the Ghetto, and, with the help of the great and valiant Lithuanian priest, Bronius Paukstys, mother and daughter were hidden in a distant peasant's home through the winter. Shulamith was quite ill at the time. Responding to pleas, the peasant family finally agreed to accept Avraham Tory as well. On March 23rd, 1944, carrying my father's last letter and testament, Tory escaped from the Ghetto and remained in hiding with Pnina and Shulamith until the German withdrawal in 1944. They returned to Kovno and were married there on August 10th. Kovno, by that time, was again under Russian occupation. The KGB knew of the existence of the documents and friends urged the Torys to surrender the material, which was endangering their safety and, possibly, their lives.

To their immense credit, and the credit of a Jewish poet and writer, Avraham Sutzkever, who urged them to hold on, the Torys did not give up or give in. Working in the dead of night, they and their friend Shraga Goldschmidt recovered with great difficulty three of the five crates from the ruins of the building where they had been buried; the other two had sunk too deep because of soil subsidence. The material was transferred to three satchels. Like a sacred text, it never left the Torys, or those to whom it was entrusted. Many months later, they were brought to Israel. The originals are still in the Torys' possession.

These, then, are the six persons who will, from time to time, appear in the tale which I am about to tell: some of these appearances, of necessity, will be very brief. I can only hope to give you glimpses of events, flashes of a searchlight. In the Holocaust, carnage goes by the name of 'Actions'. This Memoir is about the survival of people in the face of such 'Actions'.

[Following the initial German attack and the massacres of Jews by Lithuanians and Germans the Germans announced a concentration of the Jews of Kovno into a small suburb. They also called on the Jews to appoint a 'Head Jew' to speak on behalf of the Community]

The Assembly

And so, on the night of August 4th, 1941, a meeting was called at the Jewish schoolhouse at 24 Dauksos Street. Seated in the small classroom were 28 of the most trusted members of the local Jewish community. The meeting was chaired by Dr Grigory Wolff, a veteran leader of the Jewish community, director-general of Wolff Industries and head of the Central Jewish Bank.

The assembly considered a number of candidates for the position of Oberjude. None of them won general approval; some feared the risk and burden of responsibility. None of them seemed to have the strength and stature to stand up to the Gestapo or to merit the unconditional trust of the whole community, in what was clearly a matter of life and death.

Avraham Tory recalls the pall that settled over the room. It was as if the Jewish community - previously proud of the quality and abundance of its leadership - suddenly lost its way, at this most perilous moment. There was only one candidate no one was prepared to let go - Dr Elchanan

Elkes. As Tory records: 'His moral qualities, his familiarity with the German mentality, his strong bonds with the Jewish past were recognized by everyone as making him the most fitting man for the job.'

Would he succeed in carrying the burden to the end, or would he collapse under its weight? 'Modest man that he was,' writes Tory, 'Dr Elkes demurred. He said he did not have experience in public administration; he knew nothing about housing, police, public safety, work, or social service. He had never engaged in this kind of work. His field was medicine, and medicine only. He absolutely refused and asked that his candidacy be dropped.'

The leaders despaired. Little time remained and still no man of the hour had emerged. Tory continues: 'Everybody was oppressed at what could happen if we didn't appoint the people demanded by the authorities. It could only mean further bloodshed.' There was lengthy silence. And then, Rabbi Schmukler - rabbi of the Suburb of Sanciai - rose and made a statement which, in the annals of the Holocaust, has proven historic. Turning to Dr Elkes, he said: 'The Kovno Jewish community stands on the brink of disaster. Our daughters are being raped, our men are being murdered, and death is staring into our windows. Jews! The German authorities insist that we appoint an Oberjude, but what we need is a 'Leader of the Community', a trustworthy servant of the public. The man most fitting for this position at this tragic moment is Dr Elkes. We therefore turn to you and say: Dr Elkes, you may be an Oberjude for whoever wants to regard you as such, but to us you will be Leader of our Community. We all know your path will be fraught with hardship and danger, but we will go with you all the way, and may God come to our aid. With your deep Jewish faith you will take us out of the Ghetto, this exile within exile, to our Holy Land. There you will be our true leader. We implore you, be our Community Leader - Rosh Hakahal - at this time. Be strong.' And quoting an ancient Hebrew proverb, Rabbi Schmukler added, 'Remember, messengers on behalf of the Commandments suffer no harm thanks to the Prayers of the Multitude.' He closed: 'Dr Elkes, we beg of you, rise up and take over this leadership.' There was not a dry eye in the room.

Pale and serious, Dr Elkes rose. 'If you are all of the opinion that, by accepting, I will render a service to the common good, then I accept.' Immediately, the tension in the room broke. A feeling of euphoria overcame the assembly. People congratulated each other for having made such a fortunate choice. They shook Dr Elkes' hand and embraced him. They linked arms and sang the Jewish anthem, Ha Tiqva, which, translated into English, means Hope. Facing Dr Elkes, arms raised high and palms extended, Rabbi Schmukler delivered the ancient benediction: 'Go with our blessing'.

[Even after the Ghetto had been established the Germans continued to announce further restrictions. And then they proceeded to the murder of thousands of Kovno's Jews]

The Ninth Fort

Tory's next major entry is made on October 28th, 1941:

On Friday afternoon, October 24th, a Gestapo car entered the Ghetto. It carried the Gestapo Deputy Chief, Captain Schmitz, and Master Sergeant Rauca. Their appearance filled all onlookers with fear. The Council was readied and ordered the Ghetto Police to follow all their movements... Those movements were rather unusual... Instead of calling at the Council offices, they toured various places, as if looking for something, tarried awhile at Democracy Square, looked it over, leaving in their wake an ominously large question mark. What were they scheming to do?

The next day, October 25th, a Saturday afternoon, Rauca, accompanied by a high Gestapo officer, came to see the Council. He opened with a major pronouncement: 'It is imperative to increase the size of the Jewish labour force, in view of its importance for the German war effort.' He, Rauca, intends to increase the rations for both the workers and their families. To forestall competition and envy, the active labour force would be separated from the less active; those less active would be transferred to the small Ghetto. To carry out the operation, a roll call would take place. The Council was to issue an order in which the Ghetto inmates, without exception, and irrespective of sex or age, were called to report to Democracy Square at 6a.m. on the dot on October 28th. In the square, they should line up by families and by the workplace of the family head. In meeting for the roll call, they were to leave their apartments, closets and drawers open. Anybody found in his home after 6 a.m. would be shot on the spot.

The members of the Council were shaken. What did it mean? Dr Elkes attempted to get Rauca to divulge some information. He refused to add another word, and, accompanied by his associate, left the Council office.

The members of the Council remained in a state of shock. What lay in wait for the Ghetto; What was the true purpose of the roll call? Why did Rauca order the Council to publish the order rather than publish it himself? Was he planning to abuse the trust the Ghetto population placed in its Jewish leadership? If so, was it right for the Council to comply with Rauca's order; to become an accomplice to an act which might spell disaster? Was the Council entitled to take responsibility for the outcome of not publishing the order? An intermediary was contacted to inform Rauca that Dr Elkes had requested another meeting with him.

To keep the meeting secret, it took place in Dr Elkes' tiny dwelling. Dr Elkes began by saying that his responsibilities as a leader of the community and a human being obliged him to speak openly of the fears that prevailed. And since the Germans' operational intention was only to order food distribution, the Council was prepared to carry out faithfully the appropriate decree. Therefore, he went on to say, there is no need for the roll call of the entire Ghetto, including elderly people and babes in arms, since such a summons was likely to cause panic. Moreover, the three roll calls which had taken place over the past three months had each ended in terrible actions. Rauca feigned amazement that any suspicion at all could have been harbored by the members of the Council. He repeated his promise that a purely administrative matter was involved, and no evil intention lurked behind it. Dr Elkes then appealed to the conscience of the Gestapo officer - Wissen und Gewissen - hinting casually that every war, including the present one, comes to an end, and that, if Rauca answered questions openly, without concealing anything, the Jews would remember. Thus, Tory noted - as early as 1941 and, as will be seen later, not for the last time - Dr Elkes intimated possible defeat of Germany in war, leaving Rauca a way to save his skin if he helped. Rauca remained unmoved. There were no hidden plans, no ill intentions behind the decree. He concluded the meeting and left.

In the meantime, other rumours had begun to circulate. Lithuanians reported that the Russian prisoners-of-war were digging large pits at the Ninth Fort. They were labelled 'tank traps'; but when Rauca announced the roll call decree, these rumours and the roll call no longer seemed a coincidence. For hour upon hour the Council deliberated and could not reach an agreement. Would issuing the announcement be colluding with the Germans? Would not issuing the order invite savage retribution? Such was their anguish that they decided to seek the advice of Chief Rabbi Shapiro. At 11 p.m. Drs Elkes, Garfunkel, Goldberg and Levin set out for the rabbi's house. It took three meetings before the rabbi could give them counsel. In studying and interpreting his sources, he had found that there had been situations in Jewish history which resembled the dilemma the Council was facing now. In such cases, he said, he had found that when an evil edict imperilled the Jewish community and, by a certain act, part of the community could be saved, communal leaders were bound to summon their courage, take the responsibility, and save as many lives as they possibly could. According to this principle, it was incumbent on the Council to publish the decree. Reading it in retrospect, this seemed to have been the guiding principle of the Ghetto Council. If part of the community could be saved, community leaders were bound to summon their courage and their responsibility to save as many lives as possible.

Accordingly, the Ghetto Council published the announcement summoning every man, woman and child to Democracy Square at 6 am, the following morning. However, it headed the edict with the significant phrase, 'The Council has been ordered by the authorities', lest there be any misunderstanding as to the origin of the fateful announcement.

'Tuesday morning, October 28th, was a rainy day', Tory reports. 'A heavy mist covered the sky, and the whole Ghetto was shrouded in darkness. A fine sleet filled the air and covered the ground in a thin layer. From all directions, dragging themselves heavily and falteringly, groups of men, women and children, the elderly and the sick leaning on the arms of their relatives or neighbours, babies carried in their mothers' arms, proceeded in long lines. They were all wrapped in winter coats, to protect themselves against the cold. Many families stepped along slowly, holding hands, all making their way to Democracy Square. It was a procession of mourners, grieving for themselves. Some 30,000 people proceeded that morning into the unknown, towards a fate that could already have been sealed for them by their rulers.'

At 9 a.m. the Gestapo entourage appeared in the square - the Deputy Chief Captain Schmitz, Master Sergeant Rauca, Captain Jordan and Captain Thornbaum, accompanied by a squad of German policemen and Lithuanian partisans. Rauca positioned himself on a little mound. His glance ranged briefly over the column of Council members and Jewish Ghetto Police and, by a movement of the hand, he motioned them to the left, which, as it became clear, was the 'good' side. Then he signalled with a baton held in his hand, and ordered the remaining columns forward. The selection had begun.

This selection proceeded without stopping until nightfall, Rauca, from time to time, feasting on a sandwich or puffing on a cigarette. Again and again, Dr Elkes tried to intervene, responding to cries and appeals, moving this family, this group, this person from right to left. As Tory reports, 'Dr Elkes stood there, his face bearing an expression of bottomless grief. Since 6 am. this 65-year-old man had been standing on his feet, refusing to sit on the stool that had been brought to him. Now and then, when he was overcome by a fit of weakness, those near him asked him to sit down, to regain his strength, or offered him a piece of bread. He refused, muttering 'Thank you, thank you gentlemen, terrible things are happening here, I must remain standing on guard, in case I can be of assistance.' Finally, on the next day (October 29th) Dr Elkes obtained permission from Rauca to enter the small Ghetto to save another hundred people. There, however, the guards fell upon him. Savaged, trampled and beaten with rifle butts, he fell to the ground unconscious, bleeding profusely from a head wound. Jewish policemen, onlookers and Tory carried him on their shoulders into the nearest house in the big Ghetto, where he lay for three days. His head wounds were stitched, and he was nursed until he was able to return home. His effort to save a small number of Jews had almost cost him his life.

In the meantime, while he was lying unconscious, a procession numbering some 9200 people, proceeded from the small Ghetto to the Ninth Fort. It lasted from dawn until noon. Upon arrival, people were immediately set upon, stripped of every valuable article, and then forced naked into the pits which had been prepared in advance. Machine guns positioned above the pits did the rest. The murderers - Lithuanian and German - did not have time to shoot everybody in one batch before the next batch arrived. The carnage continued until the quota of some 9200 men and women and children had been met in full.

On December 1st, 1941, SS Standartenfuehrer Jaeger, Commandant of Einsatzgruppe 3, reported to his superiors his satisfaction over the completion of the initial phase of his task. Between June 22nd and December 1st, 137,346 Jews had been killed in Lithuania, among them 11 members of my family.

This Action has a sequel. In the autumn of 1943, the Germans, conscious of the Russian advance, began destroying the evidence of their killing on the Ninth Fort. They ordered the removal of the bodies from the mass graves, and their burning. A special prisoners' detail from the Ghetto – on special rations – was charged with this gruesome task.

On December 25 – Christmas Day, 1943, – following a plan conceived by a Russian prisoner, Captain Vassilenko – which involved sawing through bars over several months, forcing a lock in a storeroom door, and using white sheets to obscure footsteps in the snow once outside – 64 prisoners escaped from the Ninth Fort. Some of them found their way to the Ghetto, and subsequently joined the partisans in the Vilna forests.

Work

On October 29th, as the Germans and their Lithuanian collaborators were still shooting Jews on the Ninth Fort, not one of the Jewish slave labour brigades showed up at the gate for work. There was almost no home where someone had not been taken away – the whole community was shrouded in mourning. People no longer gave a damn. The living envied the dead. The Germans, alarmed at the sudden reduction of their workforce, ordered everybody to report, but the order was met with total apathy. This was the first time that the Germans had met non-compliance. The 'Big Action' had destroyed the illusion that work provides safety: the Ghetto and its leadership had been shaken into their terrible reality.

For this reason, Jordan and Rauca came to the Council to provide assurance, in the name of the German authorities, that the 'Big Action' was the last, and no more actions would take place. The Ghetto could enter a period of calm in which the Jews were expected to fulfil their quotas of work faithfully. This assurance was met by scepticism by the Council. But what German assurances could not achieve, hunger did.

There were only two ways of bringing food into the Ghetto, both potentially life threatening. One was to join the work brigades and trade outside, and the other was to trade through the fence. Of these, trading across the fence was by far the most dangerous. Bribes worked sometimes, but rarely. Potatoes hidden in large pockets, sacks of bread stowed away, occasionally even a half pound of sugar, a piece of bacon bought at exorbitant cost from a peasant or family: this was what trading was about.

Yet, the clearest means of survival was work, preferably work in the Ghetto. Work meant food; and the extra rations, although meagre, were extremely important. For every additional ounce of bread received on the ration card, less food from the outside source would have to be brought in or traded for. Work in the Ghetto could serve people who were too weak to march five or six miles to work and still be able to stand the rigors of hard manual labour. The Council, therefore, decided to give the establishment of workshops the highest priority. If the Germans allowed such workshops to be developed, it would increase the workforce of the Ghetto substantially. Moreover, if local German officials could enrich themselves through these workshops, they would be interested in preserving the Jewish workforce for their own benefit.

Thus, when Jordan visited the Council, the Council presented their idea to him. They stressed that the Ghetto had many first-class tailors, shoemakers, hat-makers; they could repair torn uniforms, boots, or hats for the army. Jordan showed interest. His answer came sooner than anticipated. The German rulers quickly realized the potential bonanza: they gave the Council the green light. The Council started preparations immediately. A building on Krisciukacio Street, a place where thousands of homeless Jews were housed before the 'Big Action', was assigned as a place for the workshops.

One of the first workshops to be established was one to prepare graphic displays. Graphic displays were important for the Council to keep count, and to display statistics. Armbands, signifying various work assignments, were manufactured in response to need. More importantly, the graphics department was charged with printing various edicts and proclamations, as a means of disseminating information in the Ghetto.

In the middle of November 1941, the premises assigned to the workshops were cleared and renovated. By the beginning of January 1942, the workshops started, with a tailor, a shoemaker, a furrier, and a hatter. Their first assignment was to fix 5000 pieces of clothing - suits, coats, apparel robbed from Jews during an early-hours house to house search, and, later, from the various victims of the massacres. As soon as the workshops got into full swing, the Germans started to use them for mending the uniforms of their army.

The first workshop established in 1942 was for men's clothing, operating with 12 sewing machines and necessary equipment. On January 12th, a linen sewing workshop and a brushwork workshop, employing 15 people, began operating. On January 21st, 1942, a shoemaking workshop, on February 16th, a laundry workshop; on February 16th, a soap and candle manufacturing workshop, on February 19th, a wool-shearing workshop, on March 9th, a sock-knitting workshop; and on March 10th, a workshop for children's toys; on March 10th a tinker's workshop; on March 18th, a saddler's workshop, and a workshop for processing medical bandages was also opened. Four hundred people were employed by the workshops by spring 1942. This number grew to 1800, working in shifts, in the ensuing months.

To grow food, some six acres of vegetable gardens were maintained by some 300 women. A youth movement named Eshel was established. Its members guarded the crops and ensured that they were picked and distributed fairly. Within the framework of this youth organization, young people were educated in Zionist and underground activities, while, at the same time, tending their gardens and thus feeding the Ghetto. The Germans favoured the Jews having their own source of supply; it allowed them to take for themselves the meagre rations allotted to the Ghetto. Allocation of the vegetables to inhabitants of the Ghetto was made from warehouses. Distribution throughout various parts of the Ghetto was carried out under the supervision of the supply department.

At about the same time, an elementary school was established. A clandestine kindergarten for orphaned and abandoned children was also set up. The Council also took tremendous pains in finding foster parents, who adopted orphaned children.

Ultimately, these workshops proved vital elements in the Ghetto economy, and justified the Ghetto's existence to the Germans. They also secretly supplied Jewish partisans, who fled into the forests. For that reason, the Council insisted that the workshops be managed directly by the Council, with no German interference.

And, in the jaws of death, institutions were created to maintain survival: as already mentioned, a Police Force to maintain order, and carry out the instructions of the Council; a Court, under Prof. Beliatskin, to ensure the rule of law; a Labour Office, to register, direct and protect all those working in brigades outside the Ghetto as well as within its walls; a Food Office to ensure the equitable distribution of food, either obtained from the Germans or produced within the Ghetto (this office was also charged with the distribution of firewood); a Social Welfare Office to distribute social benefits - foodstuffs, articles of clothing, money - upon proven evidence of need; a Health Office, which administered the hospital and clinic, and worked closely with both the social welfare office and the food office.

An illustration of the function of the Health Department is provided by the management of an extremely serious typhus epidemic in the autumn of 1942. Dr Brauns managed to contain this epidemic. The Germans had sustained enormous losses to typhus; and the infection, carried by lice, broke out among Lithuanian workers tending the German wounded. The conditions in the Ghetto favoured the development of infection - crowding, hunger, open cesspools, etc. News of infection in the Ghetto could have meant the instant destruction and burning of the Ghetto - just as the destruction of the Infectious Diseases Hospital on October 4th 1941 had signified the Germans' ruthless response to even the thought of contagious sickness among Jews.

A secret meeting, chaired by Dr Elkes, was held. To his immense credit Dr Brauns undertook to control the infection. He did not report the existence of some known cases of typhus to the authorities. The disease was renamed 'influenza', and Dr Brauns - obtaining special allocations of food, soap and nurses from the Council - treated 70 cases; only three died - an extraordinarily low mortality for the condition. Neither the Lithuanians nor the Germans learned what had transpired. A threat to the very life of the Ghetto had been avoided.

There was also a Housing Department, which had the terrible task of re-allocating housing as, over the months and years, the space of the Ghetto was steadily curtailed and reduced. An Office of Economic Affairs controlled the payment of moneys or distribution of articles (until all money was taken away by the Germans), a Department of Culture and Education was in charge of both the Kindergarten and the elementary/secondary schools. A Vocational School under Dr Jacob Olciski was also established. Finally, a Registration Office was charged with issuing identity-registration cards to all – everyone without exception – who made a call on the institutions and kept track of the population statistics of the Ghetto. Later, though, registration cards were falsified or destroyed to ensure the safety of people in hiding.

Yet this thin crust of life was always floating on the lava below. Though hard to believe, even deep into 1942 the Council was unaware of the enormity of the death industry in places nearby. The single radio, belonging to the Zionist underground and hidden in the cellar of the pharmacy, gave German news: it did not tell what was happening to Jews elsewhere under German occupation.

It was a report by a non-Jew, Irena Adamovitch, on July 8th, 1942, which brought home to the Council the enormous dimensions of the tragedy. Irena Adamovitch was a Polish Catholic woman, aged about 30, who had developed close relations with members of the Jewish resistance in Warsaw. In June and July 1942, she travelled from one Ghetto to another, passing information about life in the various communities. It was through her that the Jewish underground first learned of Ghettos in Poland, of Vilna, of Belsen, Sobibor, Majdanek and Auschwitz; of gas chambers and crematoria; of resistance, and partisans in the Polish forests and labour camps – an encouragement for the partisans who were gathering in Lithuania. It was people like her – non-Jews – who encouraged members of the Ghetto to identify reliable non-Jews – both lay and clergy – to establish safe escape routes. There were renewed clandestine contacts. Sometimes they worked magnificently; at others, they proved cruel traps. Children were smuggled out, hidden in sacks, among bags of potatoes, to be handed over to clergy or friendly families. The great and valiant Reverend Bronius Paukstys planned and brought about the escape of Pnina Tory, her daughter, Shulamith, and later Tory himself at the risk of his life – not once but several times over. Chief Justice Aharon Barak –

17

President of the Supreme Court of Israel and an author of the Camp David Treaty - was smuggled out of the Kovno Ghetto and kept in hiding and safety outside. As recorded by Tory and others, Dr Elkes and his Council encouraged these escapes by all means possible.

The Letter

On October 19th, 1943 Dr Elkes writes a letter to Sara and me. It is the only testament from a Council leader to have survived the Holocaust. He entrusts the letter to Avraham Tory, who encloses it in the crate to be buried last. In November, Dr Elkes requests the letter back, to add a postscript (dated November 11th) telling us of the transformation of the Ghetto to K.Z. Kauen. In January 1944, without warning or explanation, he hands the letter to Tory. On March 23rd, 1944, Avraham Tory is with Dr Elkes and – as he puts it – 'his noble wife, Miriam', in their tiny room in the Ghetto. Also present is Advocate Garfunkel. Tory's escape is being discussed. Dr Elkes is quite definite: 'If you were my son,' he says, 'I would say to you, "Go, go", for who like you knows the darkest happenings of the Ghetto? Your mission is one of the greatest importance.' That night Avraham Tory, disguised as a drover, escapes. Later he meets with Pnina, who carries my father's letter, protected in greaseproof paper, in her bra, 'next to her heart', as she puts it. She is to carry it thus for many months. The letter reaches me in the autumn of 1945.

The text of this letter, written in magnificent Hebrew, follows. Some personal passages have been omitted. It is dated October 19th, 1943:

My beloved son and daughter,

I am writing these lines, my dear children, in the vale of tears of Viliampole, Kovno Ghetto, where we have been for over two years. We have now heard that in a few days our fate is to be sealed. The Ghetto is to be crushed and torn asunder. Whether we are all to perish, or whether a few of us are to survive, is in God's hands. We fear that only those capable of slave labour will live - the rest probably are sentenced to death.

We are left, a few out of many. Out of the 35,000 Jews of Kovno, approximately 17,000 remain; out of a quarter of a million Jews in

Lithuania (including the Vilna district), only 25,000 live, plus 5000 who, during the last few days, were deported to hard labour in Latvia, stripped of all their belongings. The rest were put to death in terrible ways by the followers of the greatest Haman of all times and of all generations. Some of those dear and close to us, too, are no longer with us. Your Aunt Hannah and Uncle Arieh were killed with the 1500 souls of the Ghetto on October 4th, 1941. Uncle Zvi, (Hirsch), who was lying in the hospital suffering from a broken leg, was saved by a miracle. All the patients, doctors, nurses, relatives, and visitors who happened to be there were burned to death, after soldiers had blocked all the doors and windows of the hospital and set fire to it. In the provinces, apart from Siauliai, no single Jew survives. Your Uncle Dov and his son Samuel were taken out and killed with the rest of the Kalvarija community during the first months of the war, that is about two years ago.

Due to outer forces and inner circumstance, only our own Ghetto has managed to survive and live out its Diaspora life for the past two years, in slavery, hard labour, hunger, and deprivation. (Almost all our clothing, belongings, and books were taken from us by the authorities.)

The last massacre, when 10,000 victims were killed at one time, took place on October 28th, 1941. Our total community had to go through the 'selection' by our rulers; life or death. I am the man who, with my own eyes, saw those about to die. I was there early on the morning of October 29th, in the camp that led to the slaughter at the Ninth Fort. With my own ears I heard the awe-inspiring and terrible symphony, the weeping and screaming of 10,000 people, old and young - a scream that tore at the heart of heaven. No ear had heard such cries through the ages and the generations. With many of our martyrs, I challenged my Creator, and with them, from a heart torn in agony, I cried: 'Who is like you in the Universe, my Lord'. In my effort to save people here and there, I was beaten by soldiers. Wounded and bleeding, I fainted, and was carried in the arms of friends to a place outside the camp. There, a small group of about 30 or 40 survived - witnesses to the fire.

We are, it appears, one of the staging centres in the East. Before our eyes, before the very windows of our houses, there have passed over the last two years many, many thousands of Jews from southern Germany and Vienna, to be taken, with their belongings, to the Ninth Fort, which is some kilometres from us. We learned later that they were killed - they were told they were coming to Kovno to settle in our Ghetto.

From the day of the Ghetto's founding, I stood at its head. Our community chose me, and the authorities confirmed me as a chairman of the Council of Elders, together with my friend, the advocate Leib Garfunkel, a former member of the Lithuanian parliament, and a few other close and good people concerned and caring for the fate of the surviving few. We are trying to steer our battered ship in furious seas, when waves of decrees and decisions threaten to drown it every day. Through my influence I succeeded, at times, in easing the verdict and in scattering some of the dark clouds that hung over our heads. I bore my duties with head high and an upright countenance. Never did I ask for pity; never did I doubt our rights. I argued our case with total confidence in the justice of our demands.

In these hardest moments of our life, you, my dear ones, are always before us. You are present in our deepest thoughts and in our hearts. In the darkest nights, your mother would sit beside me, and we would both dream of your life and your future. Our innermost desire is to see you again, to embrace you, and to tell you once again how close we are to you, and how our hearts beat as we remember you and see you before us. And is there any time, day or night, when your memory is not with us? As we stand here, at the very gates of hell, with a knife poised at our necks, only your images, dear ones, sustain us.

With regard to myself, I have little to report. Last year I suffered an acute and severe attack of rheumatoid arthritis, which kept me bedridden for nine months. However, even in the most difficult days of my illness, I carried on in my community, and from my bedside participated actively in the work of my friends. Now I am better, it has been about six months since I ceased being regarded as sick. I am not fully well, either, but I continue to work ceaselessly, without rest or respite.

About six months ago we received a message from Uncle Hans, transmitted to us by way of the Red Cross, it said that you were all right. The little note, written by a stranger, took nine months to reach us. We have written and written to you by way of the Red Cross and private persons. Have any of our words reached you? We are desolate that during our stay here we could not contact you and tell you that we are still among the living. We know full well how heavily the doubt of our survival weighs upon you, and what strength and confidence you would draw from the news that we are alive. This would certainly give you courage and belief in work and life with a firm and clear goal. I deeply fear despair, and the kind of apathy which tends to drive a person out of this world. I pray that this may not happen to you. I doubt, my beloved children, whether I will ever be able to see you again, to hug you and press you to my heart. Before I leave this world and you, my dear ones, I wish to tell you once again how dear you are to us, and how deeply our souls yearn for you.

Remember, both of you, what Amalek has done to us. Remember and never forget it all your days; and pass this memory as a sacred testament to future generations. The Germans killed, slaughtered, and murdered us in complete equanimity. I was there with them. I saw them when they sent thousands of people - men, women, children, infants - to their death, while enjoying their breakfast, and while mocking our martyrs. I saw them coming back from their murderous missions - dirty, stained from head to foot with the blood of our dear ones. There they sat at their table - eating, drinking, listening to light music. They are professional executioners.

The soil of Lithuania is soaked with our blood, killed at the hands of the Lithuanians themselves; Lithuanians, with whom we have lived for hundreds of years, and whom, with all our strength, we helped to achieve their own national independence. Seven thousand of our brothers and sisters were killed by Lithuanians in terrible and barbarous ways during the last days of June 1941. They themselves, and no others, executed whole congregations, following German orders. They searched - with special pleasure - cellars and wells, fields and forests, for those in hiding, and turned them over to the 'authorities'. Never have anything to do with them; they and their children are accursed forever.

I am writing this at an hour when many desperate souls - widows and orphans, threadbare and hungry - are camping on my doorstep, imploring us for help. My strength is ebbing. There is a desert inside me. My soul is scorched. I am naked and empty. There are no words in my mouth. But you, my most dearly beloved, will know what I wanted to say to you at this hour.

And now, for a moment, I close my eyes and see you both standing before me. I embrace and kiss you both; and I say to you again that, until my last breath,

I remain your loving father,
Elchanan

November 11th, 1943

P.S.I add a few lines. It has been two weeks now since we passed from one authority to another. They have now changed our name, instead of being 'the Ghetto', we are called 'Concentration Camp No.4, Kovno', with new officials and functionaries. Our share of misery is not over yet. On the 26th of last month they took 2709 people out of our Ghetto. According to information we have received, they separated the children and the elderly - they are probably dead by now. Those who were able to work were sent to Estonia to hard labour. On the 5th of this month they took out of Siauliai all the children under 13, as well as the elderly men and women. They were told that they were being brought to Kovno. They are probably all dead now.

As to our fate, we await it in the very near future. These lines, together with some documents, I am putting in a safe place. I pray that they may reach your hands one day.

With love, affection and my blessing,

Your father

P.S. We have learned from a reliable source that the Germans are trying to erase any trace of their murders. The bones of our martyrs are to be burned in the Ninth Fort and in other places, by people who are experts in this kind of job (chemists).

Conversations

In February 1959 *Commentary* published a letter by Samuel Gringauz, a colleague from the Ghetto. The letter was headed 'Hero of Kovno' and argued that 'it behoved us above all, to preserve for generations noble images of men like Elkes'. Had my father been alive to read this letter, he would, I feel sure, have noted it with an embarrassed smile, and proceeded with the immediate business of the day. Praise and power did not sit well with Elchanan Elkes.

Yet, 45 years after his death, the memory of Dr Elkes is still fresh in the minds of some. Again and again, strangers stop Sara or me when our name is mentioned and share with us some aspect of their lives that was touched by Dr Elkes. I remember, for instance, being introduced to a guest at a party in Israel. We had chatted for a while, he not knowing who I was. Then he learned my name from someone who joined us. 'Elkes!' he said – 'Are you related to Dr Elchanan Elkes!' 'Yes, I said, 'I'm his son.' At that point, the face of this very calm, well-groomed and cultivated man contorted, tears burst forth and within seconds he was sobbing, gripping me in a helpless embrace. When he had composed himself before his astonished friends, he could only stammer, 'If only you knew what influence your father's example has had on my life.' Then he gave an instance of what he meant. 'Someone I know,' he said, 'was in Dr Elkes' office – he was seeing him on business. Suddenly, a Sturmfuehrer burst in to make demands of Dr Elkes. He put his jackboot on your father's chair. To this day, I cannot believe what happened next, for, calmly, Dr Elkes turned to the man and politely asked him to move his boot, offering him, at the same time, with cold good manners, a chair of his own. "And now, what can I do for you?" asked Dr Elkes of the SS man and then proceeded with business.'

Many of Dr Elkes' conversations are recorded by witnesses: many bear out his extraordinary reserve and presence of mind when facing his deadly enemy. A few instances will serve. In the entry of May 11th, 1943, Tory reports on an extraordinary clandestine meeting between a German officer and Dr Elkes. The ultimate intention is to bring about a meeting between Dr Elkes and Major General Heinz Jost, the feared Governor-General of Lithuania. As an intermediate step towards this contact, a meeting is to be arranged between Dr Elkes and the German judge Lukas whom, as a then lawyer, Dr Elkes had known before the war. Another contact from olden days, Dr Schtrauch (whom I remember as head of the German high school), is to be brought into the picture at a later date.

A number of meeting venues are discussed, and dismissed, and a surprising one arrived at. Lukas suggests a meeting at his own apartment. There are two reasons for this choice. First the apartment is opposite the building of the city health department; in case of need, it could be argued that Dr Elkes had entered the apartment by mistake. Second, Lukas argued that no one would suspect a German judge of inviting a Jew into his home. For additional cover, the manager of the Ghetto pharmacy and Avraham Tory would accompany Dr Elkes, but leave him alone to proceed to Judge Lukas' apartment.

In his entry Tory relates the account given him by Dr Elkes:

It was lunchtime. The table was set for Dr Elkes also. Lukas greeted him warmly, and asked him to sit at the table. Dr Elkes was seated in front of a large mirror which gave him an opportunity to observe a unique spectacle: Lukas, a judge of the German court in Kovno, dressed in the Nazi uniform, swastika on his sleeve, sat at the table opposite the Jew, Dr Elkes, who was wearing yellow badges on his clothes, on the front and back.

He proceeds:

Lukas filled two glasses with wine, and raised his glass in a toast - 'To better times.' Dr Elkes raised his glass, too, but could not bring himself to repeat his host's toast, contenting himself with a more modest response, 'To the well-being and happiness of this household.' The mirror reflected this rare scene, which inscribed itself indelibly on Dr Elkes' mind.

As for the meeting with General Jost, nothing came of it despite the goodwill of Judge Lukas and Dr Schtrauch.

In the entry for June 9th, 1943, Tory reports a meeting between Dr Elkes, SS Master Sergeant Schtitz and Colonel Karl Jaeger - both ruthless and proven killers. The overt reason is to discuss rumours concerning further actions in the Ghetto, which 'interfere with the flow of work'. The covert and real reason is to save two lives, those of Drs Nabriski and Voschin, two physicians who had escaped from the Ghetto, had been sheltered by Lithuanians and caught by the Gestapo. What follows is a condensed account of what transpired.

Jaeger receives Dr Elkes and offers him a chair, Schtitz stands to attention. 'What brings you here?' asks Jaeger. 'The fate of the Ghetto', says Dr Elkes. 'There are rumours of actions.' 'Totally groundless' replies Jaeger. 'We like to see people working. We only prosecute those engaged in sabotage or politics against us - Jew or Lithuanian.' There is some more talk. As the meeting is on the point of breaking up, Dr Elkes addresses the colonel again. 'There is another issue I wish to bring up. It concerns Dr Nabriski and Dr Voschin. Dr Nabriski is a talented physician whose services as a gynaecologist are of great importance to our hospital. His presence will ensure that women will not be absent for long periods after an abortion,' Dr Elkes continues. He has known Dr Nabriski for ten years; he is an honest man and a fine physician. Jaeger does not let Dr Elkes finish the sentence. 'Let him go', he says, turning to Schtitz. 'As ordered', says Schtitz. Dr Elkes continues, 'Dr Voschin is a young colleague of mine. I can vouch for him.' Again, Jaeger does not let him finish the sentence, but barks out the order, 'Let Dr Voschin go.'

At this point, Dr Elkes takes up the fate of the Lithuanians. 'I would also like to mention the people who have given shelter to the physicians. I am speaking to you as one human being to another. These people acted out of humane and generous impulse. They received no material reward for sheltering these two physicians. Just as a judge would take into account whether a defendant acted out of malice or greed, or out of a human impulse, so I am asking you to weigh the motivation of these people before making a decision.' 'Let the Lithuanians go', says Jaeger to Schtitz. In the hallway, the Lithuanians cross themselves and try to kiss Dr Elkes' hands. Embarrassed, he hurries on.

This visit has a sequel. On July 16th, Schtitz asks Dr Elkes to see him as a patient. Such a visit - of an Aryan to a Jewish physician - is punishable by incarceration, and even death. The visit, therefore, takes place in secret. Dr Elkes examines him and prescribes medication. 'Do you sleep?' asks Dr Elkes 'Yes', says Schtitz. 'Do you dream?' asks Dr Elkes. 'No', says Schtitz. Afterwards Dr Elkes tells Tory, 'This patient, whom destiny has forced me to check, is shocking in the extreme. Just to touch him - whose hands are covered with the blood of Jews - was horrible. Yet I suppose I did what I was meant to do. It may help to save lives.'

On May 19th, 1942, Dr Alfred Rosenberg, Minister for Eastern Affairs, with a high entourage which includes Cramer, the German city governor of Kovno, visits the workshops. At that meeting, Dr Elkes pleads for increased rations to preserve the strength and productivity of the workshops. The calm pathos of his plea, delivered in perfect German, takes the visitors by surprise. He is listened to without interruption at first. Then someone interjects: 'How dare you talk to us as if you were our equal? You are just a dirty Jew like the rest of you in the Ghetto.'

'Quite so', says Dr Elkes, 'I am a Jew like the others, and that means very much. I belong to an ancient nation, which has experienced many decrees and much suffering through the ages. However, we always knew how to overcome oppression and slavery, which have come and gone in the waves of the centuries of our existence. There is no doubt in my mind that, in this war, too, we will overcome our suffering, so as to preserve the image of God – the same God who created you and created us.'

Stadtkommissar Cramer's face is boiling as he listens. He storms out of the door leaving the other dignitaries standing.

On July 6th, 1944, Dr Elkes visits SS Obersturmfuehrer Wilhelm Goecke. The preceding months have seen terrible actions, including the children's action. The end is near.

'I am old', Dr Elkes begins. 'I have no fear of death, you can kill me on the spot. However, I have this to say to you. You listen to the radio, and we listen to the radio. You and I know that Germany has lost the war. No miracles can help you. Your patriotism cannot serve your fatherland or your party, certainly not by murdering thousands of Jews. But you can alleviate your conscience if you leave us alone. Don't supply trains for our evacuation. Postpone it until the Russians arrive. Take for yourself all the gold and valuables we still have. Leave us to be responsible for our own future. We are an ancient people with long memories and remember decency in times of peril'. Dr Elkes continues. 'Whatever your answer we will not forget.'

Goecke is taken by surprise, and listens to the end. Then, drawing himself up, he gives his reply. 'I am a German officer, and I have my orders. I cannot postpone the evacuation. I assure you, you are not being sent to die.' A relative truth, of course. The trains were meant for Stutthof and Dachau (a so-called 'Workcamp'). Dr Elkes led his people to the trains on July 13th. My mother reports that he walked firmly and erect.

Closing

I have told you a tale of life and death of a small community - a tiny statistic in the immensity of the Holocaust and the unimaginable tragedies in which our murderous century abounds. You and I will ask the same question. How is it that it survived for so long — long after other communities had been extinguished? Was there any quality to the leadership which prolonged survival? Or was it a freak of fate, a statistical play of the law of averages?

I suggest that the leadership contributed decisively to its survival as an organized community, and that the personal qualities of Dr Elkes contributed decisively to the leadership. Put simply, Dr Elkes dared, and dared from an inner and unshakeable conviction. As he writes in his last letter - the only letter, I would remind you again, from a Ghetto leader to his children to emerge from the Holocaust - 'Our community chose me... I bore my duties with head high and an upright countenance. Never did I ask for pity; never did I doubt our rights. I argued our case with total confidence in the justice of our demands.'

'Total confidence in the justice of our demands.' I have tried to project myself into the awesome loneliness of that leadership, and the extraordinary qualities it took to maintain it. Imagine – while still naïve in the ways of the SS – learning of the fate of the 534 intellectuals on the morning following the killing – and lead; of learning of the action of October 4th, 1941, which killed 1500, including his beloved sister and brother – and lead; of recovering from being beaten unconscious on the day of the action which killed 9200 – and resume leadership; being in bed for months on end, racked by severe pain – and lead; seeing through double agents, black marketers, covetousness, jealousy, false accusation – and lead; and week in, week out, facing the lying, deceiving, conniving, deadly enemy – while shouldering the full responsibility for such confrontation – and continue to lead. How many times must he have cried out for relief from his most awesome of responsibilities: the capsule of cyanide was always in his pocket. Yet, because he regarded his life as expendable, he could also use it as an asset in his dealing with the enemy. Somehow, he managed to walk through the barriers of fear to an extraordinary personal freedom.

Dr Elizabeth Maxwell asks the question, 'Why should the Holocaust be remembered and, therefore, taught?' It is not a rhetorical question. Revisionism and trivialization are afoot. The uniqueness and specificity of the event are being obscured by huge historical shifts which assault us week by week and tax to the utmost our capacity to comprehend and exercise informed judgement. Among today's fires, yesterday's fires appear less relevant. Yet no one - not even the most arrogant of intellectuals — will deny the crisis of the spirit which is abroad, irrespective of continent or nation, affluence or destitution. People, ordinary people 'We the People' as we say in America - are looking for meaning, derived not from without, but from within.

So the story of the Holocaust must be taught, not only as a stark and terrible warning for our dangerous times, but as an affirmation of our humanity, and of hope. I submit that I have told you a tale of Hope. For a community to persist and endure - as a community - in the face of the conditions which prevailed in Ghetto Kovno, sends a message which goes to that place in the heart where meaning and hope are conjoined. Hope is not disembodied. Values and belief are the sinews and substance of hope. There is a message for our times here, short and direct: 'Hold on', it says, 'it is possible.'

These qualities never left Dr Elchanan Elkes, for to him, the heart of the Jewish Ethic was the universal Ethic of Man - the 'Menschlichkeit' - of which he talked to Sara and me in our youth. I see a direct line between the Jewish officer in the Russian army who would not tolerate anti-Semitic talk in his presence, to the physician who talked of Judaism to the German and Russian ambassadors, who counselled, comforted and sustained an anguished Prime Minister, or confronted professional killers like Jaeger or Goecke in the hour of mortal danger to his community. He never was in doubt about his values, and never for one moment lost his belief in his people. Put simply, Dr Elkes knew who he was.

28

Statement by Ilana Ash, née Kamber, born in Kovno 1942

My father Marcus Kamber was enlisted into the Army on the first day of the war. He was an officer of the 16th Lithuanian Division. Before the war, my mother – Judith Moses Kamber – had worked as a nurse in the Jewish Hospital, 'Bikur Cholim' in Kovno. When the Germans entered Kovno, my mother shared the same fate as all the rest of the Jews in Kovno. She found herself in the Ghetto. Only there did she discover that she was pregnant.

I was born in March 1942 in a cellar, for it was feared that the screams of my mother would alert the Germans. I was delivered by Dr Elchanan Elkes with whom my mother worked at the Jewish Hospital before the war. Dr Elkes insisted that I be named Ilana which in Hebrew means tree, telling my mother that the new branches survive once the old tree is dead. During the first Children's Action, Dr Elkes gave me a sleeping pill and helped my mother to put me in a linen bag. My mother, pretending she had just returned from town with a bag of potatoes (at this time, they were still allowed to exchange clothes for food), had to go to the square to witness the execution of children. In this Action my 8 year old cousin was murdered. Judith Kamber witnessed how the mothers of these children lost their minds, helplessly watching their children's fate.

Once, while my mother strolled with me in the Ghetto, a German officer approached us, took me in his hands and carried me to his headquarters. My mother was convinced I was lost forever and ran around the site completely beside herself. After half an hour he emerged with me, carrying a hamper of food for us. My blond hair and blue eyes must have stirred some form of nostalgia in him.

In 1943 rumours were circulating about the possibility of another Action and the liquidation of the Ghetto. Mother began considering desperate measures to save me. Her brother Eliezer Moses had connections with underground groups in the town. He obtained the name of a Polish woman (I no longer remember the name) who helped save Jewish children. Having bribed the Ghetto guard with her wedding ring, my mother escaped with me from the Ghetto and located this woman. This woman however was to refuse me, showing my mother a room in her house full of Jewish children, mostly boys, telling my mother there was simply no room for one more child and harbouring so many children was posing a danger to them all. My mother, in a sense relieved that she could postpone our parting at least a while longer, returned to the Ghetto. But the atmosphere in the Ghetto was becoming more and more unsettling. Dates of Actions and a liquidation were already being mentioned. My mother fetched me again to the home of the Polish woman and was met once more with the same response. Out of desperation, she deposited me on the steps and said 'so be it, let her die here, she will surely not survive the Ghetto, and I will not watch her die'. The woman, convinced of my mother's resolve, took me in her arms and into her home. My mother returned to the Ghetto alone.

Thanks to my 'Aryan' appearance, a Lithuanian family living in a village not far from Kovno, adopted me. Kazis and Bronya Lutkus were a childless couple, no longer young. Naturally they had me christened and I became Laimute Lutkute. During the first few days, Bronya would take me to the Ghetto gates so that my mother could see me from beyond the gates. However, this evoked such distress and hysteria in my mother that Bronya was obliged to cease this ritual, fearing that the Germans would discover their secret. In the beginning of 1944 the Ghetto was liquidated. My mother ended up in Stutthoff Concentration Camp.

I was one of the lucky few to have ended up with caring adoptive parents. I was loved, fed and spoilt. During a walk with my adoptive mother, again, a German approached us and offered me a sweet. I thanked him in Yiddish. Bronya froze in her tracks from fear that I had inadvertently disclosed my Jewish identity. Thankfully the German failed to notice her condition; delighted, he inquired as to how I should know the German for thank-you (Yiddish and German being sister languages). From then on, I was kept at home until I forgot Yiddish and picked up Lithuanian. I read somewhere that Ghetto children developed fast. Once, playing in the yard, I noticed the Lithuanian militia approaching our house. Two messengers of the Partisans were at the Lutkus household at the time. I must have understood the danger the militia posed and ran to the gate to inform these guards that my father was not home on which they turned and left. Bronya often remarked on this event.

30

In 1944, after a serious injury and a lengthy stay in a hospital, my father was discharged from the army. He returned to a liberated Kovno. On his way from the railway station, he bumped into Eliezer Moses, my uncle, who had fled the Ghetto and joined the Partisans. Eliezer informed my father of the birth of his daughter in the Ghetto and this was how my father first knew of my existence. He immediately went to the Lutkus family and announced that he was the father. Still carrying his army kit bag, homeless (the home they had left upon being 'ghettoised' had been occupied by Lithuanians), he desired to take me back with him. The Lutkus', to their credit, advised that he should first find accommodation and work, and they would then part with me.

My father's friends, Maxim and Erica Levin, lived in a huge four bedroom house. They gave my father a room to which he brought me. Finding work also posed no problems. A Lithuania in ruins was crying for civil engineers. Father and Maxim would go to work, and Erica would look after me and Carmela, a little girl they had fostered from the Jewish Orphanage. Soon, I began calling Erica 'mama'. I spoke only Lithuanian and this remained the language I would always speak with my father, and with my mother I would speak Russian.

In 1945, survivors of the concentration camps were beginning to emerge. Father would inquire about his wife and discovered that she was in a transfer camp already in Soviet territory. He found her and brought her home. I remember nothing of my time at the Lutkus', only odd memories of life with the Levins. However, I remember with vivid clarity, the day my mother returned. It was the deep of night. Erica switched on the light in the room where I slept; I remember the violation of bright lights penetrating my eyes. She took me, somnolent as I was and carried me to the corridor,

A stranger was standing in the doorway, who, upon seeing me, burst into simultaneous crying and laughter. Erica thrust me into her arms and I can still feel the ferociousness with which she embraced me, such that I felt I was suffocating. I still remember the fear that gripped me and I was sure that I was being taken away once more. I began kicking this stranger with my arms and legs and became hysterical. Erica took me away and secured me back in my bed. I remember nothing of what happened the next day. I don't remember how I became accustomed to my mother again, I don't remember when I started to call her mama, I just know that 1 loved her very much.

In 1946, my father was appointed Chief Engineer of the Lithuanian Building Bank and we moved to Vilnius. Late one night in 1948, Bronya appeared in our home, with a two year old child in her arms. We guessed the child was adopted. Bronya told my mother that they were listed in the KGB files and were being hunted in order to be sent to exile. The husband was hiding with friends, and she was appealing to us. We were then living in a communal house with the family of a Russian Officer whose wife did not work. Bronya and the child did not leave the bedroom for a moment. Before leaving for work, my mother would leave food and a pot for them in the room, but the most difficult thing was to keep a two year old child occupied hours on end without her crying. Evidently, this could not be done. One night loud knocks were heard at the door where upon two KGB officers stormed in and went straight for the room where Bronya was staying. My father stood at the door of the room and swore on the honour of a Soviet Officer that his wife and daughter alone were asleep in this room. The Officers believed him and left. When Bronya was leaving the following morning she warned my mother if they were to get caught and should we wish to help, not under any circumstances to mention that during the war they had saved a Jewish child. In the anti-semitic atmosphere of post-war Lithuania, this would have been regarded as betrayal, not heroism.

My mother, just as other survivors of the Ghetto and the camps, spoke little of her experiences. Every time she would recollect something, she would end up in tears, smoking countless cigarettes. Not even we children survived this period without scars. I suffered from nightmares till I was 14 years old. I would awake in the middle of the night petrified and in tears. I would then be allowed to stay in my parents' bed. They were never angry with me, they always understood. Only with them did I feel safe. I refused to stay home alone until I was seventeen years old. They were always obliged to take me with them to their parties, to the cinema. The fear of losing them never left me. In those years, I was too young to understand that the trauma of the war years had not left my parents, this trauma had simply been buried deep.

I understood this only when I myself gave birth to a son Aron (Arik) in Moscow. I came to Vilnius with him to visit my father. My mother had already passed away. I could not understand how my father derived such pleasure from changing his grandson's nappy. Once he told me with regret, "I'd never had the opportunity to change my daughter's nappy, at least I get to do this for my grandson".

We emigrated to Israel in 1972. My mother's grave was left in Lithuania. She, more than anyone in our family, had dreamt of Israel. No other family members' grave exists in Lithuania. They had all been wiped out in those war years. We never found out what had been their fate. I don't know the names of my grandparents. My parents never spoke of them.

My daughter Judith, was born in Israel. She feels special because of this. She is the only one in the family who was born in her own land.

In 1999, after reading the book "Hidden History of Kovno Ghetto", I discovered that Dr Elkes who had given me my name, had children. Joel and Sara Elkes had been sent to study in England in the 1930's. I tracked them down and met with Sara who now lives in Leicester and from time to time, I speak with her brother Joel, a famous American professor of Psychiatry. In a sense I feel they are a strong link to my past. Through them at least I can express my gratitude to their father who had helped save my life.

Jewish Survival in the Holocaust

Sir Martin Gilbert

I am honoured to be asked to give the second Dr Elkes Memorial Lecture here at Leicester this evening. In my own work for more than two decades the figure of Dr Elkes has been a considerable one, certainly an inspiration to anyone who studies those terrifying years. I chose the title 'Jewish survival in the Holocaust' because it carries with it echoes of the struggle of Dr Elkes and his Council and the Jews of the Kovno Ghetto, and Jews throughout Europe in the dark years to outlive their tormentors, to live through — 'uberleben' — the fiends who were determined to destroy them.

Six million Jewish people did not survive. Hundreds of thousands, like Dr Elkes, survived almost to the end of the war only to perish in its last phase: a phase which, while full of the exuberance of imminent victory for the Allied armies and for schoolboys like myself watching from Britain as the map of German-dominated Europe constricted, was for so many Jews the time of final peril: the months of the death marches and their cruel, grim destinations: camps like Dachau and Belsen, Gardelegen and Ohrdruf, Buchenwald and Sachsenhausen, Ravensbruck and Flossenberg, all inside Germany itself, inside the continually diminishing area under German control.

The survivors when those camps were liberated often had a difficult time coming to terms with the fact that they had made it through to the victory. One of them referred bitterly to what he called 'the tainted luck of survival'. Jewish history and Jewish tradition made survival a national and spiritual imperative. 'Choose life' is one of the precious Jewish commands; it is the clarion call in the farewell address of Moses, who knew that he would not enter the promised land. In his words: 'Choose life, then you and your descendants will live'.

The nature of the Second World War created a time scale of survival that imposed itself on millions, and trapped millions. Those 250,000 German Jews who did not succeed in emigrating by September 1939 had to survive more than five and a half years of totalitarian war; Polish Jews the same five and a half years; Belgrade and Salonika Jews nearly four years; Jews in Eastern Poland, Western Russia and the Baltic States (including Kovno) more than three and a half years; Hungarian Jews, a year. Yet to survive even for a month was a struggle and a challenge, dependent not only upon one's own resources (constantly being depleted and undermined) but upon the whim and pleasure of the murderer.

When a ghetto population was taken off to an unknown destination its fate was indeed unknown. It might be a camp (like Birkenau) where some were selected to work but others, sometimes more than three-quarters of that day's arrivals, were murdered within twenty-four hours; or it might be a so-called 'Death Camp' (of which there were five: Chelmno, Belzec, Sobibor and Treblinka in German-occupied Poland, and Maly Trostenets near Minsk, in German-occupied Russia) where all the deportees, even the able bodied men, were put to death on arrival. The hundreds of slave labour camps scattered throughout the German-occupied East had their own element of irrationality. The sick and the exhausted had almost no chance of survival. For the stronger in body, or in spirit, the method of mass murder was the greatest barrier to survival: in the east, beyond Kovno, whole Jewish communities were machine gunned without mercy, shot in ditches and ravines, or in specially dug pits. At Ponar on the outskirts of Vilna, at Babi Yar just outside Kiev, at Drobitsky Yar near Kharkov, and in a hundred other death-pit locations, the chances of survival — if one lay wounded amid the corpses — were almost nil.

In war every soldier who surrendered had before 1941 certain chances. The internationally approved 'Prisoner-of-War' conventions signed in Geneva were adhered to almost without exception during the First World War. But even soldiers from 1941 to 1944, if they were Russian soldiers, had no such protection, and more than three million of them were brutally murdered, many by being put in barbed wire enclosures and left to starve or to freeze to death. If able-bodied men, trained soldiers, experienced in battle, could expect no mercy, not even what the British might call a 'sporting chance', what hope then for the unarmed, untrained Jewish civilians, deliberately confined, starved and then driven into pits.

There were Jews, too, several hundred of them, among the Polish officers put to death on Stalin's orders in April 1940: some of the leading doctors and surgeons of their time. Their pre-war medical colleagues mostly perished two years later, in the starvation of the Warsaw Ghetto. Those very doctors, themselves starving, set to work to prepare a medical treatise on the disease of starvation. Using the tragically unchangeable Ghetto starvation, they tried at least to give future generations guidance, using material that, in normal times, would not have existed, since starvation when found is treated at once with food, and the process never seen, since if caught in its late stages it can be relieved, so that the full process is averted. In Ethiopia and Somalia in the past decade, doctors worked to bring their patients back from the brink, whereas the Jewish doctors in the ghettos had to watch as the brink was passed. Recording the results, they hoped to give future medical healers at least some guidance. These noble, tormented doctors perished; their work survived.

The differing circumstances in different ghettos and villages affected survival at every stage. The Jews from the villages around Lodz were taken to Chelmno and murdered in gas vans in the first three months of 1942. The Jews of Lodz itself, with its many factories working for the German war effort, were relatively safe (after the initial deportations) until the summer of 1944 when the sudden halt in the deportations from Hungary to Auschwitz (as a result of international outcry) left the Berlin organisers with the need to fill a gap, and 40,000 Jews in the Lodz Ghetto were sent to fill it, most of them to their death; they had survived more than four years: 1940, 1941, 1942, 1943 and half of 1944.

Kovno, like Lodz, had after the initial savage, random slaughter of 1941 a place in the Nazi scheme of forced labour. It also had a remarkable leader in Dr Elkes, perhaps the most remarkable of all those who found themselves leading Jewish communities at the mercy of the sworn enemy. The leadership of Dr Elkes in its practical and in its moral aspects was a potent force for survival, unlike the leadership in some other Ghettos. In the randomness and scale of the daily mass killings, survival became a question of luck and co-incidence in Kovno for 27,000 people.

Between the German invasion of the Soviet Union in June 1941 and the end of 1941 as many as a million Jews, perhaps more, had been slaughtered in the East, most of them in their towns and villages or on the outskirts.

This was the first horrendous phase of what is now known as the Holocaust: in Hebrew the Shoah, in Yiddish the Churban. The Jews of Kovno were among the first to suffer the savagery of this unprecedented mass murder: one thousand murdered by Lithuanians on the night of June 25/26, only two days after the arrival of the German forces. Then 6,000 men, women and children taken to the 7th and 9th Forts and killed there.

Just as the Jews of Kovno had been among the first victims of mass murder, others were among the first to survive it, to find themselves with the aim, the hope, the task, the dream of living through German domination. Amid the realities of hardship the moments of hope were continuous, dependent as much upon human agency as chance, and in Kovno's case deriving in large part from the work of Dr Elkes. We are fortunate that many accounts survive of his work, not least the diary of Avraham Tory, published by Harvard University Press in 1990.

Many Jews survived from day to day in the hope of living through the time of torment to the fall of Nazism, to the day of Allied victory. But in 1941 that victory was clearly a long way off. To believe in it was, at that time, little more than an act of faith. Hitler was master of Europe, and at the gates of Moscow. Nevertheless, survival and hope went hand in hand, and with hope came rumour.

We may never know how many Jews sought survival in hiding, and how many of them perished: starved to death, or were betrayed or hunted down or gave up.

Today many of those who were hidden as children, almost all of them in Christian homes, are coming forward to tell their stories and to try to find some recognition for those who saved them. The perils of hiding were formidable, unimaginable almost for us today. I found an example from eastern Poland, in the archive at Yad Vashem (it is now printed in the diary of Harold Werner, published in 1992 by Columbia University Press). Werner was among a group of Jews who had set fire to a German storehouse on an estate that had once belonged to a Jew, David Turno:

While running from the burning estate, I noticed a bulky form crawling on all fours, like an animal, and making very strange noises. It tried to stand upright but could not, and fell back down. I pointed it out to Symcha, running next to me, and we both decided it might be a human being, perhaps a Jew. We each took hold of one arm and dragged him along with us.

The fight continued around us. We ran several miles from the estate, and then stopped to rest and look at this heap of a man. He was covered with hair down to his waist. His clothes were in shreds, and he could not stand on his feet. He looked like a skeleton and had no teeth.

From his mumblings I discovered that this being was my friend Yankel, David Turno's nephew from Warsaw. He was half delirious and did not recognise me. I understood from his mumblings that he had dug a hiding place under the feeding troughs for the cows. No one knew he was there, and he had been able to survive on the food in the troughs and the milk from the cows. He had been in this hiding place for almost a year, but the heat from the burning buildings had driven him out of his hiding place.

We continued on to the village of Mosciska, where we put him on a wagon to take him to our base. Moniek cut his long hair, and we tried to feed him, but he could not hold down any food. He was extremely weak, and a few days later he died from his malnourished state. We buried him in the woods. Afterward we grieved for what had happened to a good human being, my friend Yankel.

That Jew, Yankel, was one of innumerable Jews in hiding, who did not survive. We will never know their full number.

I have mentioned children hidden by Christians: thousands of Jews survived because of Gentile help given sometimes for money and sometimes for love of humanity. The penalties for hiding a Jew were severe - seldom less than death. The monument at Belzec records, as well as the 600,000 Jews who perished there, 1,500 Poles shot for hiding Jews. The death camp devoured them as well - we may never know their names. The names we know, of those who themselves survived, are honoured at Yad Vashem in Jerusalem. As part of the law of the State of Israel a tree is planted in their honour, and if possible they are brought to that hillside to be honoured in person.

Because of the all-encompassing nature of Nazi rule, its iron grip and its savage punishments and reprisals, those who made Jewish survival possible and survived are themselves survivors. Survival was also sought through revolt. The Warsaw Ghetto revolt of April 1943 was one of hundreds of examples of towns and villages where the Jews took up arms to resist deportation. Thousands of acts of individual defiance are also recorded – tens of thousands may never reach the light of day, for revolt was responded to by military action, by mass execution, and by reprisals on a scale unprecedented in modern times. Yet despite the virtual hopelessness of revolt, it too formed a part of the instinct of survival.

One of the leading historians of the Holocaust years – he was himself in hiding in Aryan Warsaw when he was betrayed and killed – has commented on another aspect of resistance linked also with survival. Here are Dr Ringelblum's words in his diary in 1942, after describing news that had reached the ghetto of terrible reprisals carried out by the Germans against whole streets, whole communities if a German was harmed: 'Not to act,' wrote Ringelblum, 'not to lift a hand against the Germans, has since then become the quiet, passive heroism of the common Jew.'

The variety of experience in the Holocaust is almost infinite – survival had a thousand varieties – ten thousand adversaries. We will never have a full picture – the scale of Nazi destruction ensured that we can only try to rescue from the fragmentary records of a devasted people examples of the will to survive and the courage to help others to survive.

In the late autumn of 1941 in Byelorussia a mother went into one of the vast barns of the region with her two small children. A Jewish partisan hiding in that barn was the witness. The children were both boys: one about seven, the other about four. For extra safety, as they were so small and might not be noticed in a search, the mother hid them under some bales of hay a little way off from herself. She feared she would be more easily spotted. In due course the soldiers came in, and began to search. They did not find the mother but they did find the boys. As the boys were being dragged out of the barn the younger one began to cry out, 'Mama, mama', but the older one stopped him, saying to him (the partisan heard it) 'Don't cry out "mother", or they will take her too'. And so a seven year old, about to be killed, ensured that his mother would survive at least for a little while longer.

Time, however, was against the Jews at every stage. For those hiding in the forests and marshes of Byelorussia the winters of 1941, 1942 and 1943 were still ahead of them: virtually insurmountable obstacles, especially when the harsh climatic conditions were combined with the frequent manhunts launched against them, and by the impossibility deep inside German-occupied territory of flight to a safe haven. There are even incidents (far too many incidents) of individual Jews reaching Russian or Polish partisan groups only to find that Jews were not welcome there either. It was for this reason that many entirely Jewish partisan groups grew up. Some were wiped out during the course of their activities in 1942 and 1943. Others survived and were able to greet the westward-moving Soviet forces in the early months of 1944.

One such partisan even survived, first, the death camp at Sobibor from which he escaped during the revolt; then the partisan war and then the battles in which he joined with the Soviet Army on its march into Germany. It was he (Semyon Rozenberg) who scrawled his name on the Brandenburg Gate, in May 1945, with the triumphant words beneath it: 'SOBIBOR-BERLIN'. His paean of triumph may not have meant much to most of those who read it at the time. But it means a great deal to us today.

The survivors – for such they already were – who waited liberation in the first months of 1945, had many terrible obstacles still to overcome. At Belsen (where Anne Frank perished); at Dachau (where Dr Elkes perished); and at dozens of other camps to which they had been moved from the east, the survivors of eastern ghettos and camps faced starvation and disease, and the continued savagery of their guards, including the savagery of total and inhuman neglect.

Others – several hundred thousand others – were taken out of these camps as the Allied forces approached and marched eastward again. On these death marches thousands died of sheer exhaustion or were shot down at the roadside. The victims of these death marches had survived the Holocaust, had survived earlier death marches from east to west between July 1944 (when, for example, 8,000 Kovno Jews perished on the evacuation from Kovno to Stutthof and Dachau) and January 1945, only to be murdered after the organised killing system had collapsed and after the Third Reich itself had been reduced to chaos and rubble.

One factor that always acted against Jewish survival was the Nazi obsession with killing Jews. This obsession, from the highest to the lowest in the hierarchy of genocide, saw no let-up. Even when all was lost for the Third Reich, even when every German city was in ruins, and its leader trapped in his deep underground bunker - even the suicide of Hitler on 30 April 1945, as the Red Army was fighting in the streets of Berlin - could not staunch the killing.

For the 150,000 or so surviving Jews the death of Hitler was a moment, however belated, of rejoicing even amid suffering. Here is an account of that moment by Michael Etkind, a 15-year-old survivor of the Lodz Ghetto, then in a labour camp at Sonnenberg, in the Sudetenland:

Again, there was no food. We crowded in and lay down on the straw. The guards, posted at the open doorway, sat on stools with their guns resting on their knees. They were talking quietly in their alien, Germanic tongue when someone close by overheard the words: 'Hitler is dead'.

Those three words were like a match thrown into the barn: in seconds the fire had spread from mouth to ear, from ear to mouth. And then there was a moment of silence. Suddenly, the 'Joker' - the man who'd kept the rest of us going with his humour and jokes - the man from my hut in Sonnenberg, jumped up. Like a man possessed, like a lunatic, he began to dance about waving his arms in the air; his high-pitched voice chanted with frenzy:

'I have outlived the fiend, my life-long wish fulfilled, what more need I achieve - my heart is full of joy' he sang in a transport of ecstasy. We watched him in horror, speechless. His lanky frame was swirling round until it reached the open door. No one could move. He'd run into the field outside.

One of the German guards lifted his gun, took aim. We saw the 'Joker' lift his arms again, stand up, turn around, surprised (didn't they understand, hadn't they heard, that the Monster was dead?) and, like a puppet when its strings are cut, collapse into a heap.

When liberation finally came it brought another, cruel facet to the story of survival. Not all those who were liberated in the early months of 1945 had the strength to survive the first days of freedom. Some had already perished by reason of having fixed in their minds a day by which they believed liberation would come. When that date passed and liberation, though perhaps near, had still not arrived, they perished through an ending of hope - through a savage curtailment of expectation in the immediate months before liberation. Others, survivors certainly (of five years of torment) died from the sheer, unbearable excitement of liberation, or from exhaustion and emaciation and disease that could not be redeemed by the arrival of medical care, or from the terrible richness (relatively speaking) of the food, especially the canned goods that their soldier-liberators hastened to give them (they were known in the blunt jargon of the liberated camps as the 'canned-goods victims'). At Dachau, for example, 2,400 Jews died after liberation: at Mauthausen, three thousand; at Belsen, five thousand.

My last point is one that draws me back again to the Kovno Ghetto, and to Dr Elkes. It is the aspect of survival through witness. Those who were about to die were not without one last resource: to find a way to make sure that the world would one day know the truth. The great Jewish historian, Simon Dubnow - shot dead in Riga in December 1941 - old and infirm, was said to have cried out, as he lay dying: 'Schreibt und farschreibt', ('Write and record'). It was an injunction adhered to during the Holocaust by thousands, even by tens of thousands of Jews who had no knowledge of Dubnow's words.

The young men doomed to die at Birkenau after being forced to attend to the last hours of those about to die, and their first hours of death, and then to dispose of their bodies - even they who were doomed to be killed at regular intervals - determined to set down what they could: to hide it in jars, to give witness to ensure that the truth about even the darkest corner of the black night, would survive somehow, even hidden for decades.

How well Dr Elkes understood the imperative of giving witness. He encouraged his secretary Avraham Golub, later Avraham Tory, to keep a full, day by day diary, and to hide it, together with the documents of the Ghetto, the German orders, and the Ghetto statistics. Dr Elkes also prepared his own last will and testament, which he entrusted to Tory and, with which I should like to end. It is a powerful contemporary document, not a memoir recollected long after the event, but a testimony written in the midst of the fire, one of many such that have survived, and like each of them unique. I would like to end by quoting four sections of it — and do so with great humility in the presence of the two people to whom it was (and is) addressed - his son Joel and his daughter Sara:

Joel, my beloved! Be a faithful son to your people. Take care of your nation, and do not worry about the Gentiles. During our long exile, they have not given us an eighth of an eighth of what we have given them. Immerse yourself in this question, and return to it again and again.

Try to settle in the Land of Israel. Tie your destiny to the land of our future. Even if life there may be hard, it is a life full of content and meaning. Great and mighty is the power of faith and belief. Faith can move mountains. Do not look to the left or to the right as you pursue your path. If at times you see your people straying, do not let your heart lose courage, my son. It is not their fault - it is our bitter Exile which has made them so. Let truth be always before you and under your feet. Truth will guide you and show you the path of life.

And you, my dear daughter Sara, read most carefully what I have just said to Joel. I trust your clear mind and sound judgement. Do not live for the moment; do not stray from your chosen path and pick flowers at the wayside. They soon wilt. Lead a life full of beauty, a pure life, full of content and meaning. For all your days, walk together: let no distance separate you, let no serious event come between you.

Remember, both of you, what Amalek has done to us. Remember and never forget it all your days; and pass this memory as a sacred testament to future generations.

Remember What Was Done

Professor Aubrey Newman

This evening I have the privilege of delivering what is in effect the inaugural lecture under the auspices of The Stanley Burton Centre for Holocaust Studies.

I begin by paying tribute to the vision of the family of the late Stanley Burton, who have shown themselves keen to perpetuate his memory in an academic context. He was himself a very modest man, but he was anxious to support a wide range of causes, in the field of academic life, in the arts, and in such fields as the United Nations Association and Voluntary service generally. His family's decision to associate his name with the study of the Holocaust by establishing the Stanley Burton Centre for Holocaust Studies in this University is therefore in itself a very appropriate tribute to him, and it also lays down a landmark in the study of the Holocaust in this country, for to the best of my knowledge there is no other such body dedicated to the teaching and study of the Holocaust in any other University in this country. The establishment of this Centre comes at a time when we are approaching a crucial period in the study of the Holocaust; last year, this year, and next year we will be marking the fiftieth anniversaries of a number of individual events within that overall catastrophe. We are also approaching the moment when by the passage of time we are losing the survivors of these years, those who had personal experience of the Holocaust. In consequence it is the more important that there should be such a centre. The foundation of such a Centre also raises a large number of issues about the teaching and study of the Holocaust, and I hope later this evening to draw attention to them and some of their implications.

This lecture this evening is also the third in the series of lectures in memory of Elchanan and Miriam Elkes. These lectures were established by their son and daughter not only to perpetuate the memory of their parents but also out of a realisation that what had happened some fifty years ago ought no longer be put to the back of our collective minds on the grounds that it was too horrible to contemplate; on the contrary, it was now time to convey to the next generation what had happened and what had been done in these years. That was not an easy decision for them to take, for it brought out memories which both of them would have preferred to forget. But it was taken in their understanding that their own private sentiments were now less important than the need to ensure that future generations understood what had taken place.

The first of these lectures was delivered by Professor Elkes himself; it was I know a great strain and even a moment of catharsis for both of them, and those who were there will remember it as a very moving personal tribute by Professor Elkes to his father and the work he did for his people in the Kovno Ghetto. The second lecture was delivered by Dr Martin Gilbert, the distinguished historian of the Holocaust; he reminded us of the dreadful pattern of Nazi destructiveness in Lithuania and put into a broader perspective what Elchanon Elkes had had to face. This evening in delivering the third of these lectures I want to combine these two themes, the Elkes Lecture and the formal recognition of the Stanley Burton Centre, by taking and elaborating one of Dr Elkes' own remarks and relating it to what I consider to be the work and purpose of the Centre.

In what was to be his last letter to his children Elchanan Elkes wrote:

'Remember what Amalek has done to us. Remember and never forget it all your days; and pass this memory as a sacred testament to future generations.'

'Remember what was done'...

That may seem in this day and age an unnecessary injunction. Who could possibly forget? And yet we live in an age when there are great arguments about the Holocaust. There are those who seek to deny that the Holocaust ever happened, who claim that the concentration camps are a myth, that the gas chambers are a myth, that those who died did so of typhoid or other such diseases and not at the hands of wickedness and of murderers, that the story of the Holocaust is one of a conspiracy between the Germans and the Zionists, or even finally that so far from it being a fact that six million Jews died it is all a lie, that these six million Jews changed their names and all went off happily to live in America There are those amongst these deniers who say that in any case there could not be as many

46

as six million Jews slaughtered since there were never as many as that living in Europe at the time. They claim that the camps as we see them today were all built as tourist attractions, and that if these arguments are not listened to it is not surprising, since it is well understood, they say, that all the newspapers are owned by Jews. All this would seem laughable were it not that books and articles arguing these very points have all appeared, have received credence, and that these arguments are to be found being used at this time in many countries in the world by persons who should know better, and indeed in some cases by people who do know better.

What do we do with such statements? It is tempting to say that we should be prepared to argue with these deniers and discuss their points of view. After all, we should pay respect to 'free speech' and should allow the hearing of all arguments; is that not what democracy or indeed historical enquiry is all about? These are fallacious arguments. Those who are intent on denial will not listen to reason. For those who, like David Irving, have argued that the Holocaust never happened, there ought, I suggest, never to be any platform. They are lying and indeed they know that they are lying. It is not a matter of holding any rational argument with these deniers. I would suggest indeed the inadvisability of trying to argue against them, for 'arguing' implies a degree of rationality and there is no rationality in what they are saying. By agreeing to argue with them you are even in fact suggesting that there is a discussion with two sides, and that they represent another side to the issue.

There is however the need to oppose, and, I would emphasise, a need to be well briefed, and to be able to point very clearly to the facts. It is important for example to know the distinctions between the death camps of Auschwitz, the labour camps such as Mauthausen, or the concentration camps like Dachau or Belsen. It is important to be able to distinguish between the horrors of the death factories and the equally horrific but very different horrors of Belsen or Dachau as disclosed by the advance of the Allied armies in 1945. Only by knowledge can you hope to counteract the arguments of the deniers.

There is another danger that is beginning to arise, that from the so-called Revisionists. Revisionism as such is nothing new, and in its best form is an essential part of the historian's craft, to re-examine what has happened and what has been written, and look at it from the viewpoint of the different circumstances of a different time. One feature of such revisionism developed after the first World War when many historians turned against the various forms of propaganda which appeared during and immediately after that war and showed how it was possible to argue that perhaps the Germans had not been absolutely and solely responsible for the outbreak of that war. More recently a number of historians have used this as a precedent to re-examine various aspects of the second World War, including the Holocaust, and they have suggested that German participation in that should be similarly re-examined.

These revisionists try to minimalise the dreadful events of these years; they suggest that what Hitler did is so very like for example what Stalin did in the Gulags of Russia or what was done in Nigeria or in Cambodia that it is difficult to apportion specific blame for these events against either Germany as a whole or even specifically against Hitler himself. It is, so it is claimed, what one must expect in this so-called civilised Twentieth Century, and Hitler was no different from any other of the tyrants of the world. It has been argued that while it cannot be denied that this was a war against the Jews it could well have been a war conducted against any other nation. But in fact, of course, it was not so conducted against any other nation. The Germans for example considered the Poles an inferior race, and subjected the Poles to almost intolerable tortures and degradations. On the other hand they did not issue a death sentence and track down for gassing every child of Polish descent. The industry of death which was constructed, complete with railways, death camps, gas chambers, and crematoria, was directed against the Jews and to a certain extent against the gypsies as groups; others, individuals, caught up by it were almost as it were incidental to this main purpose. While the death roll of Poles and even more of Russians is an appalling one there was never a suggestion that the Germans wished to kill every person who had Polish or Russian blood in their veins.

We are invited to participate in public debate with such revisionists, partly so as to give an appearance of academic impartiality. But such would also imply that there are in fact two sides to the discussion, and what happens in consequence is that the arguments of those who are testifying to the Holocaust are used by those who wish to deny it; the result is to give a platform to those who wish to deny or minimalise these events. It is possible to understand why many in Germany, the younger generation for example, would try to relieve themselves of the burden of a collective guilt for the second world war. What is immoral is using that set of arguments, which might or might not be legitimate interpretation, in order to defend the indefensible

One of the purposes of this lecture must be to answer some of these points, and indeed I must later on in it come back to these particular points. The first question to put is, what is it that we need to understand? We begin, we must begin, by emphasising that the Holocaust is a malignity of such dimensions that it is difficult to appreciate its scope. Sometimes one must even resort to tricks to do so. It is for example difficult to imagine six million; so in my classes I suggest this way of doing so. Count slowly to a regular beat 'One', 'Two', 'Three' etc; giving yourself a forty-hour week and a forty-eight week year it would be over two years before the beat reached six million. And that is numbers alone, not names.

If then we accept that aspect of the Holocaust, we have a problem, How far do we know what happened in the Holocaust? You must realise that so far as the Nazis were concerned all these events were to be kept secret. Right from the beginning their intention was that nothing should ever be known of what had been happening. Primo Levi reported the comments of his SS captors:

However this war may end, we have won the war against you; none of you will be left to bear witness, but even if someone were to survive, the world would not believe him. There will perhaps be suspicions, discussions, research by historians, but there will be no certainties, because we will destroy the evidence together with you. And even if some proof should remain and some of you survive, people will say that the events you describe are too monstrous to be believed; they will say that they are exaggerations of Allied propaganda and will believe us, who will deny everything, and not you. We will be the ones to dictate the history of the Camps.

And Simon Wiesenthal, another survivor, recorded a conversation he had with an SS guard nearly at the end of the war:

They would not believe you. They'd say you were mad. Might even put you into an asylum. How could anyone believe this terrible business - unless he has lived through it.

There was a continuing German insistence on official secrecy and these calls for secrecy were constantly reiterated. There was a constant obligation of secrecy laid down for all those members of the SS who took part. For example all the SS personnel who took part in Operation Reinhard, the plan for exterminating all the Jews of Poland, had to sign a guarantee of personal secrecy:

I have been thoroughly informed and instructed ... that I may not under any circumstances pass on any form of information ... on the progress, procedure, or incidents ... to any person outside the circle of the Einsatz Reinhard staff;.. that there is an absolute prohibition of photography in the camps of Einsatz Reinhard; ... I am aware that the obligation to maintain secrecy continues even after I have left the Service.

Himmler himself in addressing SS Officers in 1943 spoke of the events in Poland as 'an unwritten and never-to-be written page of glory in our history'. The German High Command had to issue orders, repeated on several occasions, forbidding members of the Wehrmacht 'to watch or take photographs of measures taken by the Sonderkommando'. And in 1942 a special unit was established by the SS with the task of obliterating the traces of execution carried out by the Einsatzgruppen in the East. During 1942, 1943, and 1944 this unit was charged with digging up mass graves and burning all corpses. Attempts were made to destroy all vestiges of as many camps as possible, so that now one can even begin to talk of the Archaeology of the Death Camps as the only way of knowing precisely how the camps and their various features were laid out.

Nonetheless, despite all the best endeavours of the murderers to keep these events secret, and despite all this emphasis on secrecy, we do have a considerable knowledge of what took place and where it took place. There were many German soldiers who came home on leave and told what they had seen or who wrote details in their correspondence home. And there were many German soldiers who against all orders took photographs of what they saw; these collections are now coming forward as evidence of what was done.

The German administration itself, as the exponent of an orderly and efficient bureaucracy, preserved masses of materials which could not be destroyed. For example, large numbers of Jews were transported by train from the various ghettos of Poland to the death camps. Like many other organisations the Germans hired special trains for a range of activities. Go today to the appropriate office of the German Railway organisation, and you will still find the accounts, fully paid by the Gestapo, all neatly filed in due order. Are there arguments over whether death camps were in fact constructed? Recent materials which have become available from the Soviet archives include the files of the Auschwitz Central Building Administration of the Waffen SS and the Police. They relate for example to the building of the furnaces. We know that the firm of Topf and Sohne made cremation furnaces for Buchenwald, Dachau, Mauthausen, and Auschwitz-Birkenau. The engineers responsible visited Auschwitz five times, between spring 1943 and autumn 1944, to inspect the machinery, to report on faults, and check whether the machinery was operating efficiently. After the war one of them was asked specifically 'Did you know that in the gas chambers and in the crematoriums there took place the liquidations of innocent human beings?' and replied, 'I have known since spring 1943 that innocent human beings were being liquidated in Auschwitz gas chambers and that their corpses were subsequently incinerated in the crematoriums.' We can point to the 'invitations to tender' sent out to these leading manufacturers, just as we can refer to their official tenders, the working drawings, and the final successful contracts, all with the firm's Logo proudly displayed on them. And with the opening of the archives of Eastern Europe even more materials have been made available. These were the papers captured by the Soviet armies or retained in the state collections of the till recently Communist states. One scholar, recently given an opportunity of examining manuscripts in Moscow, reported that he had seen twenty-five miles of shelving relating to the Holocaust - details of arrivals at Auschwitz, details of massacres in the field - all hitherto inadequately documented. He pulled out one volume at random, and found it an unknown register of deaths at Auschwitz, giving even higher totals than had been thought.

Nor are we dependent upon German sources alone. We are able to base our knowledge and our studies of the Holocaust upon documentary evidence of a very varied kind emanating from the victims themselves. When the Germans invaded eastern Europe they eventually established ghettos in which they hid away the Jews, hoping that there the Jews could be starved into disappearance or made subject to disease, and that thus their Jewish problem would be removed. There were many of these ghettos, and they varied greatly in size and purpose. But there was one feature common to most of them; there were individuals in them who made it their business to preserve records of what was happening to them. We have, in the earlier Elkes lectures, heard how in the Kovno ghetto the secretary of the Ghetto Council kept very careful notes and records of the German actions and the ghetto's reactions. But Kovno was just one of these ghettos, and all over Poland and the other areas occupied by the Germans in the east of Europe the pattern of record was the same. In the ghettos of Warsaw, Lodz, Vilna, Bialystock - the list is almost endless -we can see this desire to keep records and tell the story. Many individuals felt it their sacred duty to preserve a record. There was the venerable historian Simon Dubnow, in his eighties, who was dragged off to his death in the ghetto of Riga; one witness to his death noted that as he was taken off his last words were 'Write and Record' - 'Schreibt und Farschreibt'. In the Warsaw Ghetto those academics who were confined there set up a special research unit in order to preserve all that could be preserved. Their archive was compiled under circumstances of great danger; and when on the eve of the destruction of the Ghetto they feared for the future of their records they sealed them up and buried them within the confines of the ghetto. One of their number wrote:

I regard it as a sacred task … for everyone, whether or not he has the ability, to write down everything that he has witnessed or has heard from those who have witnessed. When the time will come, and indeed it will surely come, let the world read and know what the murderers perpetuated

Another of this Warsaw group wrote:

We reckoned that we were creating a chapter of history … What we could not cry out to the world we buried in the ground. May this treasure be delivered into good hands, may it live to see better times, so that it can alert the world to what happened in the twentieth century.

Yet another one of this group recorded his feelings:

My work was primitive, consisting of packing and hiding the material. It was perhaps the riskiest, but it was worth doing. We used to say while working - 'we can die in peace. We have bequeathed and safe-guarded our rich heritage'

I don't want thanks. It will be enough for me if the coming generations will recall our times. … I can say with assurance that this was the basis, the dynamic of our existence then. What we could not cry out to the world, we buried in the ground.

These groups then had two aims. One was somehow to let their contemporaries outside the ghettos know what was happening to them. There was a feeling inside the ghetto that nobody outside it had any comprehension about the conditions within its walls, and in consequence there was an almost overwhelming passion to tell the outside world about those conditions. If only, they felt, the outside world knew what was happening they would certainly wish to put an end to it. 'Where is Churchill?' 'Where is Roosevelt?' Almost indeed, 'Where is God?' But there was also a further desire amongst them, these historians, academics, and archivists, a need to speak not only across the gaps of space but also of time, a need to speak to future generations and tell them. In a sense we might perhaps expect to have found that sort of attitude within the comparatively settled life of the ghetto, a life where people were trying to establish some sort of 'normalcy', where there could be some hope of survival. There was some hope amongst these academics in Warsaw that they themselves would be able in due time to dig up these records and present them as a memorial of what had happened to them. Indeed, the head of the Warsaw group, Emanuel Ringelblum, actually set up his archive in the hope that eventually it would be used not only as the basis for historical research but as legal evidence against the Germans. As a consequence every single activity of the Germans against the Jews of the Warsaw Ghetto had to be recorded and preserved. But if this part of their hopes were to be disappointed, if they themselves were not to be able to present their evidence, then at least the material would talk to the next generation, at least their own sufferings would not have been in vain. Someone therefore eventually would know despite all the attempts by the Germans to keep their activities a secret.

In addition to these official or quasi-official records we have also in many cases a wide range of what has been termed survival literature, that is the individual diaries and testaments of what their writers went through in the ghettos. Some of these authors survived the ghettos to tell their stories and, indeed, there are even those who went into the death camps and survived to tell the world what had happened to them and others.

The works of Primo Levi or Elie Wiesel are but the more prominent examples of this genre of literature. From them we have only too clear a set of descriptions of what life was like in Auschwitz or Treblinka or others of the camps set up with the sole purpose of destroying life as effectively as modern industrial techniques could envisage. Those who survived had a compulsion to write, even if only to purge themselves of the guilt of having survived where so many others had died. Elie Wiesel questions why he wrote:

Having survived by chance, I was duty bound to give meaning to my survival, to justify each moment of my life. I knew the story had to be told. Not to transmit an experience is to betray it.

Primo Levi records his own attitude towards life after his liberation:

I was living badly. The things I had seen and suffered were burning inside of me; I felt closer to the dead than the living, and felt guilty of being a man because men had built Auschwitz and Auschwitz had gobbled down millions of human beings ... It seemed to me that I would be purified if I told its story, and I felt like Coleridge's Ancient Mariner, who waylays on the street the wedding guests going to the feast inflicting on them the story of his misfortune.

Many of these survivors could not cope with survival. Psychiatrists have recognised deep-seated problems amongst the survivors, many of whom, such as Primo Levi, eventually decided that they had to make an end of their torments; even the children of the survivors have felt this same guilt and the same traumas. But in addition to these works written after the event, what might ironically be called emotion recollected in tranquillity, there are other very moving testimonies. In each of the death camps there were groups of prisoners given a temporary reprieve. These were the members of the Sonderkommando, such as those in Auschwitz, given the task of clearing the corpses from the gas chambers and conveying them to the crematoria, clearing the ashes from the crematoria and dumping them into the great ashpits. Their reprieve could only be a temporary measure; few of them were to be given even as long as six months to exist by their German masters. Each of these groups in their turn were put to death, and their places were taken by another group, equally doomed to eventual death. But they too had an overwhelming desire and need to tell their story. Some of them wanted to join friends and relatives in the gas chambers, only to be informed by these victims that as they had even a remote chance of life they had a duty to try to live and to bear witness. But those, particularly those in Auschwitz, as it became clearer that the Germans were losing the war, they felt that their lease on life was ebbing away. They were clearly not to be given an opportunity of testifying as to what they had seen and experienced. And so they set down on paper, at enormous risk and pain and effort, what they had seen and experienced, and then they carefully buried their notes in a wide variety of containers actually amongst the ashes thrown out from the crematoria. When the Russians came to the Auschwitz death-camp at the end of the war they began to find these messages out of the ashes. Let me quote one of them, which still speaks as vividly as the day it was found:

Dear finder, search everywhere, in every inch of ground. Dozens of documents are buried beneath it, mine and those of other persons, which will throw light on everything that happened here. Great quantities of teeth also are buried here. It was we, the commando workers, who deliberately strewed them all over the ground, as many as we could, so that the world should find material traces of the millions of murdered people. We ourselves have lost hope of being able to see the moment of liberation

Let me once more quote from Dr Elkes' last letter, with his description what he had himself seen and experienced: "The Germans killed, slaughtered, and murdered us in complete equanimity. I was there with them. I saw them when they sent thousands of people - men, women, children, infants - to their death ... I saw them coming back from their murderous missions - dirty, stained from head to foot with the blood of our dear ones."

Nor can there be any doubt about the way in which in a sense the perpetrators prepared for what might be argued in the future. In 1943 a Yiddish poet interned in a French camp wrote: " They will not believe that Hitler's nation prepared and carried out the slaughter of seven million Jewish souls. They will not believe it - and worse they will pretend to believe the 'Big Lie' this filthy nation has used throughout the war: we did not kill the Jews. The Jews died on the way to the concentration camps."

There can be no argument then as to the facts of the Holocaust. We have a great deal of information, and a feeling that those who suffered are in a way passing on almost a trust, that we are almost as it were duty-bound to listen to them. And it raises also the issue as to whether, having listened to these voices, we ourselves have any right not to pass them on to another generation, to teach that generation how to understand how and why these events occurred. I have heard, as I am sure many here have heard, the question, 'Is it not time to forgive and forget?' That is almost a theological question, and one which I for one am not qualified to answer; but let me suggest that the only ones qualified to forgive are those who themselves suffered; if I see someone else being assaulted before my eyes have I the right to say to the criminal 'I forgive you?'. Equally let me affirm that we, as historians, do not have any right to forget. To understand, yes; to comprehend, yes; but not to ignore and not to remove from our collective memories.

And so now, either in terms of this lecture or even in terms of various developments in teaching the Holocaust, this seems to be an appropriate time to take stock, to take this Elkes Lecture, to link it with the establishment of the Stanley Burton Centre, and then to discuss the issues involved with the teaching and study of this subject.

I said earlier that there are issues to be raised about the teaching of the Holocaust to the next generation. If this evening my main theme has been that of 'the need to remember' we have some obvious problems. Obviously we are losing those who can remember the Holocaust from their own experience , and there is a generation with no personal contact at all with its horrors. How can we 'Remember' when we have nothing in our personal consciousness to which we can relate? Clearly before we can remember we must have something to remember. If the new generation is to remember they must learn, they must be taught what it is they have to remember. Inherent therefore in the desire to 'Remember' is the need to teach, and I would argue that a commitment to ensure that the Holocaust is to be remembered involves also a commitment to ensure that it is taught.

Some years ago I was in America, teaching at a University in the mid-West and I can still remember the horror shown then by a very venerable gentleman when I asked him, 'who now remembers Kishineff? And in

56

forty years time will people remember Auschwitz and Dachau?'. Almost certainly I have to explain this evening that some ninety years ago Kishineff was the scene of the official massacre of some 30 plus Russian Jews, and that the horror at such an event travelled the whole world. It raised much more horror at the time than the massacres some forty years later. He was appalled that anyone had forgotten Kishineff. And it occurred to me, talking to that gentleman, that many would be distressed at the thought that after a hundred years such names as Dachau or Auschwitz might equally well be forgotten.

And therefore when my colleagues in the Department here in Leicester urged me to include a study of the Holocaust as part of our syllabus I was prepared to agree. It was not a subject which I like teaching; indeed let me say that I hate doing so. Indeed I am not sure how fitted I have been to teach it. I think that I would be the first to say that I am not and never have been a true scholar of the Holocaust. My research and my studies in depth do not lie in this field. In my Inaugural Lecture some six and a half years ago I dwelt upon the reign of George II and I have still a book only half-completed in that field. So far as the Holocaust is concerned I am a teacher, a communicator, fitted to initiate such studies, to encourage others towards them, and what I have published in this area has been in terms of how and why I have been teaching this subject.

But I have had to teach that subject, and once you are involved in it you have problems. Again to quote Elie Wiesel, 'We are all obsessed. That is the special impact that this world, the world of Auschwitz has on us. ... As scholars, as writers, and commentators. Once you enter it ... you are no longer the same person; you are inhabited by its fire.' And so I have had to teach it, and I have tried to teach it without dwelling on horrors for the sake of horrors, and I have taught it because I feel that for me there is no alternative. But I would do so only on what I considered to be conditions - not conditions laid down by me to the Department or laid down by the Department to me. These were conditions laid down by me to myself. This was not a subject to be approached in a highly emotional frame of mind. This was to be a proper subject for historical analysis, and in that I have been greatly assisted by the nature of teaching here at Leicester. It so happens that over the years that I have taught it here I have had only one University undergraduate who was Jewish. All the others have been non-Jewish; indeed I have had sitting in on classes

57

on one occasion a number of German students here on exchange programmes, and it would have been discourteous at the very least to have imposed upon them highly charged, emotional attitudes. And indeed it would have been unnecessary, for the facts speak loudly enough for themselves.

The other factor in this teaching, which has increasingly become important, as it was one of the conditions I laid down for myself, has been to make the documents speak for themselves. We have studied texts, the voices of those who suffered, the voices of those who imposed suffering, and above all the precise, clinical tones of a bureaucracy intent on finding so-called solutions to what they thought of as problems. That has been what has made this course here at Leicester unique in the country and what I hope for some time to come will continue to give it its distinctive nature. Nowhere else, in the teaching of the Holocaust, do students pay the attention to texts as our students do here.

I feel very strongly that the events of these years must be looked at within two contexts. They must be set firstly within the context of European history in general, as part of a study of the ways in which Europe developed as a whole, with its nationalisms, its strains. and stresses as well as discussing the structure of a small minority striving to live in an outside world, striving to understand that world and be understood by it. The second context must be within the context of Jewish history as a whole. It is inexcusable to look at these events as merely a series of martyrdoms, as if Jewish history could be represented only in terms of massacres and pogroms. Certainly so far as Eastern European Jewish history is concerned a civilisation had grown up in Eastern Europe which was to be destroyed by these incursions, and only if the nature of that civilisation and way of life was understood by those studying the Holocaust could it be fully comprehended. And in that connection I feel very strongly that those who come to the study of the Holocaust purely through the study of German history need to be reminded continuously that the bulk of the victims were not Central Europeans but Eastern Europeans.

Each year I ask my students, why they want to study this subject in great depth. They have no personal links with it. After all, they were not alive at the time nor do they have relations who suffered in these years. Their answers never cease to amaze me, for they have an acute concept of the continuing relevance of these years. They produce work which shows remarkable insights; last year one of them produced a seminar paper on women in the death camps, and I had to confess to her that I did not know how she had had the heart to read it to the class. Her fellows were affected just as much as she had been. But it goes somewhat deeper, for there is amongst them a feeling of immediate relevance. It is not just a realisation that there has been a revival of Neo-nazi feeling all over Europe, not least of all in Germany. The fact is that what happened then could happen again, if not exactly in the same form then something nearly like it. I am asked whether there could be another Holocaust, and in the narrow sense there could not. Hitler did his work too well, and with the destruction of over six million Jews there are not enough Jews in Europe to form the basis of another Holocaust. But in a broader and more general sense the issues are still relevant. Santanyana once declared that those who do not remember their history will be forced to relive it. When we look around at this time can we be absolutely certain that there is no immediate relevance to a study of these issues? When for example we see the continued racial hatred in Germany against foreign workers, Turks who after three generations of living in Germany still cannot legally acquire German citizenship, does that not invite various comparisons. The Nuremberg laws in 1935 stated clearly that only those of German blood could become German citizens.

Even so the question still remains as to why we should at this time be persuading, even encouraging students to take on board the study of these dreadful events. We might well ask simply, 'What is to be the purpose of this Centre and what will it be trying to do over the years?' In general terms the aim of the Centre must be to promote the study of the Holocaust at both an undergraduate and graduate level, but also it must go out and convey to the general public why what we are trying to do is of importance.

Obviously so long as there is undergraduate teaching of the Holocaust here in Leicester the Centre and its Honorary Director will have to be involved, and here just as I must thank the very many people, members of the Anglo-Jewish community and others, who have enabled me to raise the sum of £150,000 as a token of a commitment to these studies so I must also thank the University of Leicester for having accepted that token and in taking on that burden making available the additional resources which have made possible the appointment of an established member of staff to do precisely this. But the Centre must be more than that. The Burton family has been generous in establishing the Stanley Burton Centre, and their aim has been through the Centre to foster the future study of the events of these years. I see the work of the Centre following three paths. It will continue the work of undergraduate teaching of the Holocaust for so long as that plays a significant part in the syllabus of the Department and of the University. But undergraduate teaching is not enough in itself; if the Centre is to fulfil its task and to make its mark, if indeed it is to repay the University for the support which the University has been giving it, it must move forward into the area of research. It must promote research, and invite scholars to participate in seminars both here in Leicester and on a national scale. It would be wrong to try and work on our own, and it is important to cooperate with whatever has been established on a national basis, as well as with other institutions and Universities, such as Birmingham or Warwick, Southampton or Keele operating regionally. We would not wish to try and have a monopoly in this, and all are welcome. The work of research has already begun, and one of the paths of research which we are already trying to foster is an understanding of how the newspapers and the radio reacted to the various pieces of news about the Holocaust as they came drifting into Britain during these years, and to try and see to what extent the general public were made aware of what was happening; and if not, why not. Such studies have obvious links with, for example, the work of our own Centre for Mass Communications Research as well as with other groups interested in research into what I might term 'The Media'. But even the desire to foster academic research into the Holocaust both in this country and elsewhere is not enough. There must be a third angle to the work of the Centre It will have to be conspicuous in the desire to reach out to the wider non-academic general public, children and adults alike, and teach them, to remind them of what happened to the Jews of Europe. We are just seeing the release of the film Schindler's List; it will be said that that film will demonstrate the truth to those who deny the Holocaust. It will not. A film will not in itself change the opinions of those who deny. But those who do not know, or those who have not thought, will be affected. Those who go to see it and those who having seen it realise that these are things that were done and the persons portrayed were not cardboard cut-outs but real persons, they are the people who will be affected by it. We hope also to sponsor the publication of a series of Survivors' Testimonies, where those unpublished accounts of what was done can be preserved and made available for as wide a public as possible. We hope also to build up a substantial collection of resource materials, to establish a Resources Centre for the study of the Holocaust, and in that connection we have already received the first donations towards the establishment of a specific Holocaust Centre Library, a collection of books from Dr David Rosenberg in memory of his wife, the late Patricia O'Keefe.

Equally, as a further part of our activities, we hope next year to mark the fiftieth anniversary of the liberation of the camp at Bergen-Belsen, to hold a conference with as wide a public audience as possible. In 1945 the reports from horror-struck war correspondents opened the eyes of the general public to the atrocities of these camps - and these were far from being the worst of the camps - so we want to remind the general public of what they felt then.

Fifty years from now there will be generations with no direct link with the victims of these events. It will be almost inconceivable that there should be no remembrance of them. But if there are to be such remembrances, and if they are to be more than merely formal rituals, if those participating are truly to commemorate what was done, it is our duty to pass on, to twine together the two threads I have been trying to twine together this evening. But let us not do this in any wrong headed spirit. Our duty to remember is not something confined to any particular religion or even group in society. Those who do not remember their history will be condemned to relive it. I would quote the words of one survivor, Ben Helfgott.

No-one in the world … can really convey what we felt, what we experienced … So that those who died will not have died in vain we must be constantly aware of what happens when a government or people take it on themselves to decide the fate of other people.

There is too often too much of a desire to ignore, to deliberately forget, to pretend that nothing happened, and to allow all memory to die. And there is therefore a greater need to overcome these feelings.

Ladies and Gentlemen, Dr Elkes' command 'Remember what was done' was not an instruction just to his children. Through them is an instruction for all of us. And here I am not addressing just one religious community, the representatives of those who suffered particularly in these years; what was done then is a matter that affects all of humanity – – it affects those who suffered, it affects those who inflicted the suffering, and it affects those who stood by and let the suffering occur. As John Donne wrote, 'Ask not for whom the bell tolls'. There is the guilt of the by-stander just as there is the guilt of the perpetrator. But I would go further with Dr Elkes' command; it is an instruction not just for his own time, but, I would suggest, an instruction that has validity for generations to come. So that if we see such horrors again be it today, tomorrow, next year, in twenty years time that command should still remain relevant. And therefore in 'Remembering What Was Done' we are reminding ourselves of certain values and we are teaching others of the importance of those values. I am grateful therefore to all those donors who have helped in providing the means by which we can continue to implement that instruction for the future. I am grateful to the Elkes family who have this evening given me a platform. I am grateful to the Burton family who have contributed the framework which will make possible the continuation of this work for the future. And, above all, I am grateful to the University which over the past years has made it possible for me to carry out my own part in its implementation.

Killing Time: Jewish Perceptions During the Holocaust

Michael R. Marrus

University of Toronto

A little child said today: "I do not yet wear the armband, but when I grow up I will wear one." A fine portent.

— Adam Czerniakow, October 11, 1941[1]

In a remarkable short story the Israeli writer Ida Fink, a Holocaust survivor of Polish-Jewish background, suggests that Jews who suffered the full onslaught of the Nazi horrors developed a peculiar sense of time, different from everyone else. "We had different measures of time, we different ones, always different, always with that mark of difference that moved some of us to pride and others to humility." This different sort of time was "not measured in months and years," she notes, but in her case at least was marked by a word - Aktion - denoting the roundups of Jews in the small towns and ghettos in which they lived just before being murdered. "(W)e no longer said 'in the beautiful month of May,' but 'after the first "action," or the second, or right before the third." One day, in one of her short stories, a young girl like the author watched in horror and fear from a slope overlooking the assembly-point for the victims, and saw the men and older boys loaded onto trucks and taken away to be shot. Recounting that day, the narrator notes that her perception of time changed. "We sat there for an hour, maybe two, I don't know, because it was then that time measured in the ordinary way stopped."[2]

This essay takes up Ida Fink's preoccupation with time in an effort to explore Jewish responses to the Nazis' murderous onslaught against them. In so doing, it follows an investigatory path of other historians who have examined other eras, and other problems. It considers changing perceptions of time as a reflection of social and cultural transformation, as did Gustav Belfinger a century ago in a pioneering work on the

63

passage from the medieval to the modern era.[3] It looks at notions of time as a way of coping with a crisis situation, as did Jacques Le Goff in a study of artisan workers in the fourteenth century.[4] And it looks at a rich variety of ways of measuring and experiencing time, as did Emmanuel Le Roy Ladurie in his study of the village of Montaillou, divided as it was at the end of the Middle Ages between Christian and pagan, secular and ecclesiastical, urban and rural, artisan and peasant, and many other ways of life.[5]

In keeping with Ida Fink's story, I will limit myself to the perceptions of Jews facing intense persecution, arrest, deportation, extreme privation or murder. For only in these circumstances, as I will try to make clear, did the Jewish victims' perception of time distinguish itself as so extraordinary. This means that my focus is on Nazi-occupied Europe - leaving aside Jews in neutral countries, in the tiny Yishuv in Palestine, or in various other places of refuge. Seeking "Jewish time," I appreciate that the latter Jews' views of the world were informed by special Jewish anxieties and fed by distinctly Jewish channels of information. But Jews outside the Nazi prison were generally not cut off, and did not measure time so consistently differently from their non-Jewish neighbours as to warrant the kind of discussion I want to pursue here. Jews in Palestine may constitute an exception to this remark, but since their own situation was so different from Jews elsewhere it is probably best to consider their perceptions separately.[6] Finally, I refer only loosely to "Jewish time," for I do not want to attribute to the many kinds of Jews discussed here any single notion of time deriving from Jewish tradition. My focus is on Jews caught in the Nazi Holocaust, and their circumstances, of course, were remarkably diverse.

That said, it is never entirely clear with whom to begin, and when perceptions of time may be deemed to have been special in the sense that Fink understands. It is very well known, for example, that many German Jews did not immediately grasp the great threat Nazism posed to their existence. Understandably enough, many of them shared the views of so many non-Jewish compatriots in the mid-1930s that Hitler was a passing phenomenon, that the Nazi Party would not maintain its hold on government for long, and that the Jews' suffering would soon be eased. Joachim Prinz, one of the leading rabbis in Berlin and a colleague of the Rabbi Leo Baeck, recalled how this argument was put by a prominent member of the Jewish community using an analogy of time: "The tower and the clock are right here in this country," he said, "And if I read it well, it is not midnight at all. Tomorrow will be a new day, and someday the hour will strike, and we will be free."[7]

"Unfulfilled expectations or hopes are invariably called illusions in retrospect," observes Roderick Kedward, a historian of the resistance movement in southern France.[8] We should take care lest we denigrate the perceptions of Jewish optimists, deeming their sense of time as wildly unrealistic and contradicted by evidence that could be plainly seen. At least in some cases optimism involved a determined effort to put things into perspective, to look beyond an immediate present. And that is why it sometimes infuriated Nazi persecutors. In the mid 1930s Rabbi Ernst Appel of Dortmund spoke some comforting words at a Jewish funeral in the countryside. After the ceremony he was interrogated at the police station: "How can you dare, you dirty Jew, tell your people that they should hope for a better time to come?"[9]

For German Jews, as indeed for Jews everywhere when they first experienced Nazi persecution, understanding their circumstances required an assessment of time – usually accompanied by anguished debates. Would the Nazis remain in power for long? Would the persecution of Jews diminish, or might it quickly worsen? Were the military victories of the Reich definitive? Or would the Allies eventually throw the Germans back? Some Jewish leaders in positions of responsibility felt duty-bound to express the long view. On April 1, 1933, Robert Weltsch, editor-in-chief of the Zionist newspaper the *Judische Rundschau,* published his famous editorial, "Wear the Yellow Badge with Pride!" in response to the Nazis' boycott of Jewish businesses. "The first of April, 1933, can be a day of Jewish awakening and Jewish rebirth," he wrote, "if the Jews want it to be".[10] In Weltsch's view, and in the view of so many other leaders who tried to comfort and sustain their people during the Holocaust, Nazi persecution was to be understood as one more in a long chain of persecutions extending back throughout history. "We remember all those who were called Jews, stigmatised as Jews over a period of five thousand years," Weltsch wrote at the conclusion of his article. In the same spirit, Rabbi Leo Baeck composed a special prayer for all Jewish communities in Germany on the eve of Yom Kippur, October 10, 1935: "Our history is the history of spiritual greatness, spiritual dignity. We turn to it when attack and insult are directed against us, when need and suffering press in upon us. The Lord led our fathers from generation to generation. He will continue to lead us and our children through our days. . . our way is clear, we see our future."[11]

Ordinary Jews evaluated time in the context of their background, temperament, and their immediate, personal experience. Many searched their own past as they pondered the present. "I am a creature of the Great War," wrote the Rumanian-Jewish physician Emil Dorian in 1938, with the historical perspective of so many middle-aged European Jews. As such, Dorian was a pessimist, "my soul rent by fear and revolt, my thoughts darkened by awareness of death and the uselessness of all endeavour." [12] Some contemplated the Nazi present through the prism of ideology. For the celebrated writer Stefan Zweig, as with so many other educated German Jews in 1933, his Jewish identity was fused with liberalism and universalism. "One cannot easily dispose of thirty or forty years of deep faith in the world inside of a few weeks," he wrote in his autobiography.[13] Emigration was agony for Jews such as this - leading to suicide in Zweig's case; no matter where they were, wrote Jean Améry, like Zweig of Austrian background, German-Jewish émigrés were "still spinning the thread of destiny of the German nation."[14] But others were more sanguine. Zionism set a different timetable, with its leadership, at least, urging a large-scale exodus to Palestine in short order. And Revisionist Zionists went furthest of all - in the case of Germany challenging mainstream Zionists for moving too slowly, and urging the complete liquidation of German Jewry through rapid emigration.[15]

To emigrate or not to emigrate? Jews debated the matter with great intensity, turning their arguments frequently on the question of time. Definitely not, said the banker Max Warburg in 1933, determined to defend his family's banking firm "like a fortress," as he later put it. While Warburg was convinced that Jews were about to suffer a period of suffering, as he later explained, "it was my firm belief that this period would be limited in duration."[16] Emphatically yes, said others who also claimed to have the long view. "What good is it to stay and to wait for the slowly coming ruin?" one émigré remembered the argument that was presented. "Is it not far better to go and to build up a new existence somewhere else in the world, before our strength is crippled by the everlasting strain on our nerves, on our souls? Is not our children's future more important than a fruitless holding out against Nazi cruelties and prejudices?"[17] Some championed emigration without any sense of urgency, maintaining that there was plenty of time to leave. After consultation with Max Warburg a British Zionist group produced a memorandum on emigration in 1935 envisioning departures over a four-year period of Jews aged seventeen to thirty-five, ultimately reducing German Jewry by half.[18] Through the mid-1930s German Jews debated the direction to be taken in newly-energised Jewish vocational training centres. Some saw these ventures as emergency preparation for leaving Germany; others insisted on a long-term restructuring of Jewish life in which vocational training played only one role. And until the end of 1937, historian Avraham Barkai reminds us, a large proportion of German Jews believed there was a long-term future for Jews in Germany.[19]

Debates about emigration and the outcome of the war usually reflected varying assessments of time. Some who fled insisted on remaining close to Germany, expecting to return home quickly, as soon as Hitler was overthrown. Stefan Zweig arrived in London in 1934, and was reluctant to sink roots. "I did not take a house but rented a little flat, just big enough to accommodate the two book cases."[20] Max Warburg and his wife sailed for New York in August 1938, confidently expecting to return in the autumn to resume the direction of several charitable enterprises in Hamburg.[21] He never saw Germany again. Two years later, seemingly unable to commit himself to leave France, torn between his patriotism, family commitments, and uncertainty about the future, historian Marc Bloch procrastinated, swinging between optimism and pessimism in assessing the future.[22] Similarly motivated by a powerful French patriotism, Raymond-Raoul Lambert, the future head of the U.G.I.F. for the unoccupied zone, refused to believe that the French defeat of June 1940 was definitive. "La guerre continue. Attendons," he wrote in November. Periodically, Lambert was full of expectation that Nazi Germany would soon collapse. "Je pense que je reverrai Paris en automne 1942," he wrote in July of that year. "Les bombardements Anglais se multiplient en Allemagne." A few months later he concluded that a German victory was impossible, although her defeat would be long postponed. But by December he dared to hope for a victory in the following year. And so he continued until his deportation - electrified with hope from time to time, convinced that the end was just a few months away.[23] Optimism, in this optic, was a patriotic duty - a commitment to the triumph of liberal and republican values over the dark forces of Nazism and the persecution of the Jews. Under German occupation, these patriots had to admit, many had resigned themselves to the Vichy government's order of things and believed the Nazis' New Order would continue indefinitely. "J'ai foi, cependant, dans une evolution plus rapide des événements," Lucien Vidal-Naquet confided to his diary in December 1943. Faith, as much as anything else, shaped this optimistic notion of time.[24]

Very different was the state of mind of those who did get away and who understood their departure as definitive. These were generally refugees of a later vintage than Stefan Zweig, many of them leaving under exceptionally difficult personal circumstances. Convinced that time was short, facing a level of persecution unknown in Germany in 1933, robbed of most of their possessions, hounded from office to office to collect the necessary documents, these Jews understood that a Jewish chapter in the places in which they had lived was closed forever. For them, there was no turning back. Edwin Landau described his emotional collapse before his family when his arrangements to depart were finally complete: "The children either did not know or did not understand why I was crying so violently, but I knew: this was my leave-taking from everything German, my inner separation from what had been my fatherland - a burial. I buried forty-three years of my life."[25] In 1938, with the passing of the Racial Laws in Italy, sixteen-year-old Dan Segré left for Palestine in a wrenching departure from a country in which his family was both prominent and wealthy - and included among them a prominent Jewish Fascist. "I broke my ties with the Italian nation," he wrote in his memoirs, "in a series of secret, night-time ceremonies, during the course of which I buried, under the great cedar of Lebanon in my mother's garden, my black Fascist dagger, a wooden tomahawk, and my collection of tin soldiers - the symbols of my now-shattered hopes of joining the Royal Military College."[26]

For Jews who remained behind, persecution imposed new preoccupations with time. Curfews and other temporal restrictions made clear distinctions between Jews and non-Jews, for example, and required Jews to reorganise their lives accordingly. Following Kristallnacht the German government empowered state and provincial authorities to set limits on the times in which Jews could appear in public, and with the outbreak of war they were ordered to stay at home between eight p.m. and six a.m. The authorities also limited the times in which Jews could shop - usually in the afternoons, guaranteeing that they would not have access to scarce foodstuffs and some rationed items. Two years later the decree forcing Jews to wear a yellow star facilitated enforcement of these regulations.[27] Throughout Europe, curfews and restrictions such as these went hand in hand with the German occupation, with local authorities defining the rules and setting penalties - usually very severe, including deportation and death - for failure to comply.

Like other civilians in wartime Europe, Jews spent much of their time in queues, waiting endlessly for food or for official authorizations for one thing or another. Thinking of these and other constraints on civilian life Leonard Woolf wrote of the "negative emptiness and the desolation of personal and cosmic boredom" of war.[28] But special curfews and other temporal restrictions, together with the dangers for Jews of appearing in public for sustained periods of time for any number of reasons, were additional burdens that complicated the lives of Jews extraordinarily and forced some to the brink of starvation. In his diary of wartime Paris, for example, Jacques Bidinky dwells obsessively on the time he spent lining up for food. Nearly five hours for some charcuterie and a few cans of conserves, he notes on December 5, 1940: four hours for a bit of cheese on December 31; an hour and a half for an egg on February 10, 1941; three hours for 400 grams of veal, including bones on May 10; four hours in front of a charcuterie on June 12, for nothing at all; four hours for two kilos of potatoes on August 24. And then, on October 31, 1942, the Commissariat général aux questions juives announced that Jews could only shop between eleven and twelve in the mornings.[29]

One should not underestimate the strain that waiting imposed upon Jews, and the menace of curfews defined precisely for them - whether they were living among non-Jews or forced together in teeming ghettos. Immediately after conquering Warsaw the Germans set a curfew of seven p.m. (later changed to eight) for civilians, but as Chaim Kaplan noted, even before special restrictions on Jews the latter felt it too dangerous to remain on the streets after six. Jews, Kaplan observed, "shut themselves up in rooms within rooms, with drawn shades and extinguished candles, listening for the echo of footsteps reaching them from beyond the door." And he then added to his diary: "I swear that I neither distort nor exaggerate."[30] Before the ghetto in Warsaw was sealed the Germans adjusted the curfew for the entire city, setting it at eleven for non-Jews and seven for Jews; meanwhile, Jews inside the newly-established ghetto were allowed to be outside until nine. Little wonder that – as the Nazis no doubt intended – there was some appeal for Jews to move into the ghetto where restrictions seemed easier to bear. Both inside and outside ghettos, however, time constraints involved a daily round of rushing about to meet appointed hours – shopping, working, and meeting the curfew at the end of the day – with a failure to meet each appointment and each deadline involving dreadful consequences – hunger, inspection of identity documents, arrest, impressment into work gangs, and the danger of being murdered.[31] Diaries and memoirs of Jews who picked their way through these minefields of restrictions are replete with references to curfews – rumours about their being extended, adjustments by the occupation authorities, petitions from Jews to have them extended, and so forth.[32]

Outside the framework of curfews, rhythms of time differed dramatically for Jews in hiding or eking out a pitiful existence within the framework of the strict isolation imposed upon them by the Nazis or their collaborators. Common to almost all of them were long periods of intense boredom – an experience of the passage of time we seldom associate with Jews during the Holocaust. "Nothing ever happens here," wrote an elderly Jew from a small town in the Rhine valley in 1940, when there were fewer than a dozen Jews left of a pre-Nazi community of about 150. "Here there is one day like the next. Nothing changes... I am well but weary of life, I am now old enough."[33] Too old to emigrate, unable to start a new life for themselves, lonely and cut off from their neighbours, such Jews endured long periods of emptiness before the end finally came. Young people suffered similarly. Shortly after moving into the "secret annex" with her family, Anne Frank marvelled in her diary about how she had changed: "Who, three months ago, would ever have guessed that quicksilver Anne would have to sit still for hours —and what's more, could?"[34] Anne filled her day with studies – "time-killing subjects," she called them – in a conscious effort to fill in the hours. "We have nothing else to do but make the days go by as quickly as possible, so that the end of our time here comes more quickly."[35] And with the boredom went irritation. "Hiding in other people's homes meant not only losing touch with the world outside, but also putting up with irksome restrictions and constant danger," wrote Janina Bauman, of her months spent living with a Christian family in Rembertów, not far from Warsaw. "Confined to a limited space, doomed to idleness, we seemed to have no life of our own. . . . Our existence was blank, we just marked time."[36]

For many Jews in hiding time stood still, as they found themselves suspended between a world they had known and the secret (to them) world of the non-Jews around them. Banished at the start of the Abyssinian War (1935) to confinement in a small, primitive village in a remote region of southern Italy (admittedly as an opponent of the regime, not as a Jew), Carlo Levi described a universe of patience and resignation with a culture, dialect, world-view and conception of time utterly different from anything he had known — "that closed world, shrouded in black veils, bloody and earthy, that other world where the peasants live and which no one can enter without a magic key."[37] How to make the time pass in an utterly alien environment? Debórah Dwork combed memoirs and the recollections of survivors of what the Germans called U-Boot Juden, Jews living illegally, sometimes in hiding places, sometimes under false identities, and sometimes on the run, literally walking the streets all day. Children studied; adults made bric-a-brac, puttered about, and passed books from hand to hand. In the Netherlands, Philip Maas and his parents passed much of the time thinking about food. In the Ukraine, hidden away in a pigsty, Moishe Koblansky and his family devoted a good part of the day to killing lice.[38] Irritable, the fugitives sometimes quarrelled bitterly with one another. For all of them the challenge was to maintain equilibrium in the face of an exquisite void. Not everyone, of course, could do so. Some burst the bounds of enforced idleness, leaving a shelter, emerging into the open in search of something better, even agreeing to be "resettled." Ida Fink calls these "the Impatient Ones" — "doomed to destruction by their anxiety and their inability to remain still."[39]

The ghettos of Eastern Europe are a unique laboratory for the study of time, with their teeming populations of Jewish inmates, all of them cut off in some sense from the non-Jewish world. Forced together, living in terrorised but distinct Jewish republics, many ghetto inhabitants speculated about their place in historical time —using language and concepts replete with what David Roskies has called "archetypes of destruction," taken from Jewish history. He refers to the familiar landmarks of Jewish trials and tribulations: "the burning of the Temple (the sacred centre), the death of the martyr (the sacred person), and the pogrom (the destruction of the Holy Community) — were all alive in the minds of common people and intellectuals alike, even those emancipated from religious practice, due to the folk and modern literary responses to catastrophe that had evolved since the 1840s."[40] And so this is a common theme of ghetto diaries and memoirs.

In his chronicle of life in the Warsaw Ghetto, Emmanuel Ringelblum reports the inhabitants' preoccupation with historical time. "There's been the growth of a strong sense of historical consciousness recently," he notes in November 1940. "We tie in fad after fad from our daily experience with the events of history.... The Jews created another world for themselves in the past, and in living in it forgot their troubles around them...." And in June 1942, Ringelblum returns to the subject in a discussion of what people in the ghetto were reading. His answer was history, and particularly the history of warfare: Jews were reading about Napoleon Bonaparte, notably his campaign of 1812 in Tsarist Russia, Tolstoy's War and Peace and works on the First World War — accounts of the downfall of the so-called "invincible" powers. "In a word, being unable to take revenge on the enemy in reality, we are seeking it in fantasy, in literature. This explains our preoccupation with previous wars, which we turn to for a solution to the tragic problems of the present war."[41]

Other witnesses note the ghetto inmates' association with the Jewish past through religious observance or the calendar of festivals. Visiting a forcibly closed mikveh (ritual bathhouse) in Warsaw, for example, Shimon Huberband imagined "the sight of our forefathers in Spain — how they rescued Torah scrolls, how they prayed with a minyan in secret cellars, due to the fear of the Inquisition."[42] Purim celebrations associated the downfall of Haman with that of Hitler; the Jewish New Year linked with a call for Jewish redemption. Passover was a particular time to meditate upon the plight of the Jews — their enslavement and eventual salvation — as Avraham Tory noted in his description of a clandestine seder in Kovno, ending with the singing of "Hatikva" (Hope), the Zionist hymn. "The atmosphere was so enthusiastic and hearty that we were loathe to disperse," he wrote. "There were dances which lasted long into the night." Note the date: April 26, 1943.[43]

Within the ghetto there were endless debates over time — juxtaposing divergent evaluations of how long the war would last, whether rapid transformations were possible and how long the Jews could hold out — frequently referring to the spring, when the hardships of winter would be past. Optimists suggested that time worked in favour of the Jews. When the Warsaw Ghetto was first sealed, we are told, some Jews told non-Jewish friends, "come visit us next week" — expecting that the measure was only temporary.[44] Ghetto diarists record whole series of similarly optimistic speculations, mixing rumour with wishful thinking and scraps of facts, extending from 1940 or 1941 to the moment before the ghetto's final remnants were deported and murdered. In these assessments the Germans had been thrown into retreat, Hitler had been overthrown, the Reich was about to collapse, and so forth. But just as strong were the opposing views — that the end was far off, and that the Nazis' empire would remain strong indefinitely. Complicating this debate between what Abraham Lewin called the "shorteners" versus the "lengtheners," was the realisation that the final stage of the war might be the most dangerous of all, and might well precipitate the liquidation of the ghetto. A longer war, some reasoned, might preserve the ghetto or at least a remnant, for an indefinite future. The debate was nothing if not complicated, with optimists easily becoming pessimists, and pessimists optimists.[45]

In some cases the leaders of the Judenrate, the Nazi-imposed Jewish governing authorities in the ghettos of eastern Europe, took the most awesome decisions resting upon assessments of time. Sometimes unwillingly, and frequently bludgeoned into doing so, these leaders co-operated with the occupying authorities, acceded to demands to supply workers for the Nazis' war machine, and sometimes even helped to round up some of the ghettos' inhabitants for deportation and eventual murder. A frequent defence of this policy was that working with the Germans bought time — a transaction that, in the end, might save at least some of the ghetto inhabitants. "The Jewish police rescued all those who had to live," Judenrat chairman Jacob Gens of Vilna protested in October 1942. "Those whose days were close to the end in any event had to go. And may these aged Jews forgive us, they were the sacrifice for our Jews and our future." "I want to postpone the Aktion so as to gain time, which is so valuable for us," Gens is quoted as saying — this at the end of August, 1943, several weeks before his own murder and the destruction of what was left of the ghetto. "Time is on our side. I am convinced that the Soviet Army will reach Vilna by December of this year, and if at that time the ghetto still survives, even though a few will be left in it, I shall know that I completed my task."[46] Chaim Rumkowski, the iron-willed Jewish autocrat of the Lodz ghetto, seemingly carried away by a messianic vision of his own indispensability, made the same calculation in an awful speech on September 4, 1942, justifying the rounding up of the elderly, the ill, and children under the age of eleven. "We were not.., motivated by the thought of how many would be lost, but by the consideration of how many it would be possible to save," Rumkowski said. His policy riveted on a vision of the future — a postwar era in which Jews surviving Hitler would resettle the surviving Jews and in which he, Rumkowski, would play a major part.[47]

In a more benign effort at utilising time, the Judenrate invested Jewish energies and communal resources in numerous projects that looked to a future, as if assuming, sometimes in the teeth of the evidence, that Jews should reasonably plan ahead. Officially, they presented themselves to their communities as optimists. In the long run, so the argument went, many Jews would survive. In this respect the Jewish authorities in ghettos acted similarly to Jews outside ghettos in West and Central European countries, with the principal difference being the scale of their activities and the degree to which they were able to act in the open. Two quite different illustrations may suffice — education and vegetable gardens — although I should underscore that these are susceptible to differing interpretations.

In a way that might seem astonishing to us, the ghetto authorities built remarkable school systems, designed not only to keep children and young people busy, but genuinely to educate, seemingly in calculation that time had by no means run out. The Warsaw Ghetto, for example, had an elaborate network of schools religious, secular and Zionist — with some 6,700 pupils enrolled at the end of the 1941-42 school year. More than 2,300 students were also involved in vocational training.[48] Debórah Dwork notes how ghetto schools provided companionship for the students, and also helped support the teachers, many of whom had no other source of livelihood.[49] And time was also a consideration. Yitskhok Rudashevski, a teenager in Vilna, wrote in his diary how he ached to resume his studies. "When I used to go to my lessons, I knew how to divide the days, and the days would fly, and now they drag by for me grayly and sadly." But once he began classes in the ghetto gymnasium, the world changed. "The day passed quite differently. Lessons, subjects.... We waste less time, the day is divided and flies by very quickly.... Yes, that is how it should be in the ghetto, the day should fly by and we should not waste time."[50]

Students like Rudashevski did not simply fill in the hours. One notes not only the time spent in teaching and study, but also the writing of examinations —the sign, as every student knows, that the process is a serious one. Rudashevski's contemporary, fourteen-year-old Janina Bauman from Warsaw, recalls labouring over translations from Horace and the theorem of Pythagorus in an underground study group begun on the students' own initiative. In the middle of June 1942, shortly before the massive deportations from the ghetto, and with starvation, disease and misery all around them, she and her fellow students wrote their examinations — "unofficial," the punctilious Bauman now remembers, since the students could be evaluated by their own teachers only.[51] (I am struck by how, looking back, candidates for these exams remember small details, as examination candidates universally do. In Amsterdam, seventeen-year-old Bloeme Evers Emden, for example, took high school examinations in twelve subjects at the Jewish Lyceum just before receiving a deportation notice. Having passed the written exams, she was set for the orals — normally held over two days, six subjects a day. In view of her prospective deportation the school's director agreed to compress the exams into a single day. She passed, received her diploma that afternoon, and was picked up by the authorities that very evening.[52]) Examinations were one more landmark in the passage of "normal" time, and the need to maintain that, whenever possible, may have been the most powerful motivation of all. "I felt that I must play normal," one student in the Warsaw Ghetto's underground medical school recalled. "Everything is normal, otherwise I couldn't exist."[53]

Vegetable gardens, as every gardener appreciates, also involved calculations of time. Of course, gardening in the ghettos paralleled the gardening by civilians everywhere in war-torn Europe, and was the most obvious way of supplementing a pitifully inadequate food supply. Because of the catastrophic situation in the ghettos, however, there was much more desperation than elsewhere, and hence an intense collective interest in the tiny plots that were available. Some Judenrate, as in Lodz, for example, had special departments of agriculture to oversee the crops, down to the monitoring of individual plants in order to protect them against premature harvesting.[54] But notwithstanding the collective efforts, starvation in some cases forced the cultivation schedule. In Kovno, vacant land under cultivation amounted to 25 dunams (about six acres) in four different locations, cared for by a corps of 300 women. A trained agronomist, Shlomo Kelzon, was in charge, with surveillance and distribution provided by a Zionist youth movement known as Eshel (a Hebrew acronym for Organization of Garden Guards).[55] Despite the guards, however, ghetto inmates constantly threatened the crops before they were ripe. Because of a shortage of wire and planks the fields could not be fenced off, and during the summer of 1942 starving inhabitants of the ghetto pilfered the vegetables. The Judenrat struggled to preserve what was left over the entire growing season — demanding that the starving, in effect, wait.[56] In addition to matters of public concern, ghetto diaries and memoirs reveal extraordinary preoccupations with time in daily routines, amusements, and interpersonal relations — the sinews of life in these doomed communities. Essentially, these were strategies for living of people who realise that there may have been little time left. One point to note is the dreadful pressure of daily living, the struggle to keep alive, worry about loved ones, the strain to meet obligations. Life in the ghettos — one senses this in the rare film footage that has survived —involved a perpetual rush to accomplish the tasks of daily life. Smuggling, barter, sales of food in markets — all of these had to be done in great haste, either to avoid detection or to secure one's hoard in the face of theft or scarcity. Working shifts were long — nine, ten, then twelve hours a day — leaving only a short time before curfew to scrounge for food, fuel, and other necessities.[57] And in every memoir or diary there is the shock of new disaster — a roundup, a massacre, or some impossible new regulation. Simply moving about on the streets could be dangerous, leaving one exposed to random attacks, arrest, or roundups for work gangs. Hence more reason for haste. Right down to the very end, when the ghettos were being liquidated, the diarists betray an obsession with time in their daily existence. In August, 1942, as tens of thousands were being deported from the Warsaw Ghetto, the young David Graber, aged nineteen, wrote his testament, which was buried in the Oneg Shabbat Archive. "We must hurry, we know not our time. At work until the last moment."[58]

For those with the most vitality, one encounters a further reason to rush —to get the most out of life while it lasts. Some inhabitants managed even to find time for partying. Chaim Kaplan and other writers comment on frivolity within the ghetto — music, dancing, and so on — "in order somewhat to lessen its sorrow."[59] Janina Bauman remembers a party of about thirteen young people, with records and vodka. Because of the curfew, they all spent the night in an apartment together. One of the boys approached her friend Zula. "In a fatherly way he told Zula that with life as it is we shouldn't wait for our true love before making love, because we might never live that long."[60] Ida Fink tells a heartbreaking story of a thin, dark-haired girl assigned to a labour gang, working on the Ostbahn. It was a good assignment, Fink writes, because the Aufseherin (guard) was someone the workers knew who allowed them an occasional break in the surrounding forest. The girl in this story spent every free moment devouring a battered copy of Romain Roland's famous novel, *Jean-Christophe,* for which there was a great vogue at the time. She was always in a rush to get on with her reading. "I have to hurry," she said. "I want to make sure I finish it in time... .I'm afraid I won't have time to finish it."[61]

Across Europe, those Jews engaged in organised, active opposition to Nazi policies — ranging from armed revolt to rescue of every sort — had very particular preoccupations with time. As observers of all underground movements know well, resistance everywhere desperately needs time — time to recruit, time to win over some of the surrounding population, time to find hiding places, time to accumulate weapons and resources, time to train fighters and other operatives, time to link with allies, time to gather intelligence, and time to formulate plans. But Jews everywhere lacked time, as the Nazis pounced on them with their full weight and ferocity, sometimes in the first moments of occupation. For reasons largely beyond the Jews' control their efforts were always, even in their own estimation, too little, too late — even though they struggled into action at a time when many other civilians had barely managed even to contemplate resistance activity. According to Emmanuel Ringelbum, for example, the leader of the Warsaw Ghetto insurgents told him that he deeply regretted that two years had been "wasted" on educational and cultural work. Once armed resistance was decided upon, the rebels realised first and foremost how time was short.[62]

Like most underground movements, the Jewish resistance spent most of its energy simply trying to remain undetected. Leaving aside the dangers from the Germans or their auxiliaries, for example, armed bands of Jewish partisans faced a staggering challenge just to get through the winter months without freezing or starving to death. In the description of Herschel Zimmermarin, horizons of time were closely bound to the daily struggle to stay alive: night time, when the fugitive-fighters could move about undetected; early morning hours before sunrise when it was the coldest; daytime, when they needed shelter and sleep. Long-term visions in the winter were of the spring, when the partisans would not leave tracks in the snow and when they could come out of the woods for a bit, prowling closer to villages and farm communities.[63] Spring was a time when the ground defrosted, and when potatoes, buried in the fields by peasants to use for seed, could be dug up for food. "There is nothing that could have cheered us more than the first sign of spring," write some veterans of the struggle. "We knew we had survived the worst and better days were ahead. We had much less to worry about."[64]

Resistance strategists ruminated endlessly on the key issue of strategy: When was the right moment to strike? In his diary, Avraham Tory elaborated:

how should we act in the case of a partial "action" in the Ghetto, or in the case of an attempted total extermination of its residents, or in the case of a total evacuation of the Ghetto? What would be the right moment to hide away in various hiding places? When should we cut the barbed-wire fence for a mass escape? Should we go to the forest or try to look for shelter in villages? How should we establish contact with the outside world? From where would come the resources necessary for carrying out our plans? When should we act alone, or should we take our families with us?[65]

For political reasons, some urged rebels to wait. The Jewish Bund, in 1942, wanted to postpone an uprising in order to forge links with the non-Jewish left on the other side of the ghetto walls. Others wanted to act more quickly, before it was too late.[66] But because of the furious reprisals the Nazis exacted for every action, taking their dreadful toll of the entire community, timing was a moral question as much as a political calculation. Abba Kovner was one of the leaders of the rebels in Vilna and participated in such debates. "As regards revolt," he recalled, "we cogitated more than anything else over the moral aspect. Were we

78

entitled to do this, and when?"[67] In the spring of 1943 he and his comrades produced a document on the subject of timing which they appended to their official "Combat Regulations." "Premature action is tantamount to frivolity," it said, "an action taken too late — a crime." In the end, the Central Command would decide.[68] After anguished consideration in Warsaw, the leadership of the Jewish underground decided that the enemy, by his own actions, would determine the right time by betraying an intention to liquidate the ghetto; then, and only then, would fighting begin. "We waited for the Germans to dictate the time and place of our uprising," writes Yitzhak Zuckerman, deputy commander of the Jewish Fighting Organisation. "We hoped we would be ready in time."[69]

Resistors were forced to think about the nature of the struggle once engaged, how long it would last, and what were its goals. In Warsaw as in so many other places, the Jewish Fighting Organisation saw its struggle in part as a symbolic act in time, a fight to the death. "We knew that we were going to die. The question was only when and how to finish," Yitzhak Zuckerman recalls.[70] He and his fellow fighters envisioned a short spasm of violence and never contemplated holding out for weeks — hence they did not prepare caches of food and looked askance at elaborate hiding places.[71] In this vein, Jewish resistors frequently pointed to the impact of their struggle upon posterity. Virtually all of them were making an appeal to history. Theirs was a national struggle, "to defend [the Jew's] life and honour," as the Vilna partisans put it, with the appeal emphatically to the future.[72] "Zog nit keynmol," the partisan hymn written and composed by the twenty-three-year-old Vilna poet Hirsh Glik and which has been taken as an anthem for the Jewish resistance during the Holocaust, returns to this theme in several verses:

Never say that you have reached the very end,
Though leaden skies a bitter future may portend;
And the hour for which we've yearned may yet arrive,
And our marching step will thunder: "We survive!"

From green palm trees to the land of distant snow,
We are here with our sorrow, our woe,
And wherever our blood was shed in pain,
Our fighting spirits now will resurrect again.

The golden rays of morning sun will dry our tears,
Dispelling bitter agony of yesteryears,
But if the sun and dawn with us will be delayed,
Then let this song ring out to you the call, instead.[73]

Can one speak of the Jews' sense of time in concentration and death camps, at the end point in the continuum of human misery which marks the history of the Holocaust?[74] In a penetrating essay, Primo Levi once took up the question of the intellectual in Auschwitz, part of his polemic with a fellow survivor of the camp, Jean Améry. Levi showed a certain impatience with Améry's ruminations on culture and theorising in Auschwitz — even when it came to the subject of death.

Life, or at least the bit of it that prisoners still grasped in Auschwitz, was simply too demanding. "I almost never had the time to devote to death. I had many other things to keep me busy — finding a bit of bread, avoiding exhausting work, patching my shoes, stealing a broom, or interpreting the signs and faces around me." "The day was dense," he says elsewhere.[75] To be sure, there was a wide variety of camps— transit camps, work camps, as well as the most dreadful instances on which I want to concentrate here, and so my view is not only a summary but also a partial one. But I think it makes sense to dwell upon the worst cases, to speak of the limits, if it may be put this way, to consider approaches to time that differ substantially from those already discussed in this lecture.

As Levi suggests, many prisoners were too numbed to have any temporal sense at all. For many, the ability to delineate time was practically obliterated in the deportation convoy before they even reached their destination. In his remarkable book, *The Long Voyage,* Jorge Semprun portrays the excruciating hardships of these human transports. Sealed in the darkness, jammed together, without food or water, the prisoners travelled for days. At the end, half-dead, they were utterly disoriented. Semprun, himself a former deportee, describes "the sticky dough we had all become, all hundred and nineteen anonymous mouths, until the final burst of despair, of nerves completely shattered, the last vestiges of self-control exhausted." How many days and how many nights had they spent in transit? "(I)t's all terribly confused. . . everything is more or less hazy."[76] Even those with the luck and the strength to survive the first shock of arrival — the dogs, the lights, the noise, the whips, and the selection —

even these hardy survivors could be engulfed by the challenge of getting from one moment to the next. Many were simply crushed, with no sense at all beyond the awesome present. Elie Cohen writes of "a narrowing of consciousness" in the camps, so that inmates focused attention on one single aim, self-preservation.[77] Some, indeed, believed they were finished. "You know you're going to die," a survivor recounted years after, attempting to convey his thoughts at the time. "Your brain is telling you you're through, you're dead. You're just walking, but you're dead now. I was sure I was dead now."[78]

Once installed in the camp those who had survived the initiation conformed to routines marked strictly by the clock — imposed time, one might say, since no prisoner could own a watch, and the only demarcation of the hours came from the gong or whistle or siren or the shouts of the kapos that sounded periodically throughout the day. (To be in possession of a timepiece indeed, likely meant one was planning to use it in an escape, and to be caught with a watch meant a sentence of death.)[79] Like so much else, time in camps was hoarded by the authorities and dolled out to suit the soul-destroying, murderous purpose of the place — "just enough sleep at night to work during the day, and just enough time to eat," noted one survivor.[80] Prisoners were awakened at four or four-thirty in the warm weather (an hour later in the winter), took their meagre rations, went to the toilets (ten minutes or so in Birkenau, one historian observes, for 7,000 inmates, many of whom suffered from diarrhoea or dysentery, to negotiate a narrow latrine barrack 118 feet long, with doors at each end, with space for 150 inmates over an open sewer), and then rushed to their work — constantly driven by the kapos who insured that no one slackened the pace.[81] In contrast to this hurrying was the often excruciatingly drawn-out roll call — standing in formation to be counted, sometimes for hours on end, out of doors, exhausted, freezing in the cold, drenched by rain or sweltering in the sun, waiting for the mindless task of counting (both the living and the dead) to be completed. The most rigid routines, therefore, in which time itself was meted out as a punishment, nearly always too much or too little —part of the mind-numbing torture, as virtually all prisoners remember. And scarcely any other time seemed to matter. "For us, history had stopped," says Primo Levi.[82]

Routines were not frozen, however, and were subject constantly to sudden interruptions of schedules and unexpected impositions of new things to do. Prisoners dreaded these changes — selections, for example, assemblies to witness floggings or hangings, alterations in work assignments, or transfers to other camps — for these posed huge risks, and meant death more often than not. "'When things change, they change for the worse,' was one of the proverbs of the camp," Primo Levi tells us. This was one more reason for an obliteration of a sense of time. The prisoners learned "the vanity of every conjecture: why worry oneself trying to read into the future when no action, no word of ours could have the minimum influence? ... our wisdom lay in 'not trying to understand,' not imagining the future, not tormenting ourselves as to how and when it would all be over; not asking others or ourselves any questions."[83]

Change usually involved waiting: to have one's number called, to be selected, to get orders — or simply waiting for no apparent reason at all. Prisoners' memoirs frequently dwell upon the process — the long queues, the monotony of standing in line, and especially the mind-chilling fear. "Waiting in fear is surely one of the most awful of human tribulations," writes British novelist Iris Murdoch. ..... "The sheer extension of time is felt then as physical anguish."[84] "Waiting in fear" describes much of the Jews' experience of time during the Holocaust, of course; nowhere was this more ghastly, however, than it was for Jews who believed it was possible, or even probable, that they were waiting for their own deaths. This sometimes happened outside the camps; only there, however, was such waiting practically "routine." "People laboured under a continual anxiety of expectation," Wolfgang Sofsky notes.[85]

Jews in camps were uniquely cut off from a normal sense of time, in the opinion of Elie Cohen, because they had no idea of how long they would remain imprisoned, and generally no sense of whether any relatives or friends who linked them to the past were still alive.[86] For that matter, they had no knowledge of how much time remained in the working day — not to mention what the next day would bring. Virtually all of the familiar temporal landmarks had been taken away. With shaven heads, without their own clothes, having lost even their names which had been exchanged for numbers, and with many or most of their relatives killed, these Jews were uniquely cut off from their own past. Isolated in camps — or even sections of camps — they were also cut off from the historical present. Information about the war trickled into places like

Auschwitz with the arrival of new prisoners, but only some had access to it, and in any event it was not easy to grasp and appreciate. To be sure, some prisoners found the energy to hope for liberation, but a more constant preoccupation was to get through the next few hours, the day, or the week. In the winter, some hardy souls capable of a long-term vision, thought in terms of months, looking to the time when the sun would warm their bodies and dry the earth. "Today, in this place, our only purpose is to reach the spring." Primo Levi remembers thinking. "In a month, the cold will call a truce and we will have one enemy less."[87]

Despite this narrowing of consciousness, some Jews managed to articulate a historical sense of time, a heroic achievement under the circumstances one might say. "If the Germans win the war, what will the world know of us?" mused the Polish writer and Auschwitz-survivor Tadeuz Borowski, conveying the nightmarish question that occurred to him and to other prisoners as well.[88] In his survey of the literature of concentration camps Terrence Des Pres writes of the commitment "to bear witness" common to so many survivors, to which we should add the urge of some, even in the torture of camp existence, to survive precisely in order to tell the tale — bespeaking an orientation to historical time and a determination to leave a mark. Filip Muller, a Jewish worker stoking one of the crematoria at Birkenau, was handed some testamentary poems by two girls as they entered the gas chamber: "You stay alive and tell the world what happened to us," they told him. For similar reasons, Jewish rebels in Auschwitz buried tracts in canisters to be read after their deaths.[89] Jewish artists did the same, seeking a vehicle to communicate to a future world what the Jews had endured. Zoran Music described the sense of urgency with which he sketched in Dachau: "I was in a febrile grip. Tomorrow may be too late. For me, life and death depended on these sheets." "We wanted to be among the living at least on paper," explained the Auschwitz slave labourer Halina Olomucki.[90] With what motivation? Revenge? Jewish survival? Or a "faith in human continuity," the "foundation of humanness," as Des Pres hypothesises? It is hard to be sure, and it doubtless depends on the individual. But of the urge itself there is no doubt.

Most Jews were neither artists nor writers, and left no trace of their deepest reflections on what they had endured. Their innermost feelings — different for every individual — were locked up inside them and destroyed by the Nazis as part of their murderous campaign. Still, they had some thoughts and experiences that were shared and which historians now attempt to reconstruct. And among such shared thoughts and experiences, I have tried to point out in this lecture, was the Jews' sense of time. Of course, Jews understood time as their particular circumstances, opportunities, luck, and personal commitments dictated. Their sense of time varied considerably. In some cases, it may not have differed much from their non-Jewish neighbours, many of whom suffered terribly under Nazism. But Ida Fink still has a point. The Jewish victims had extraordinary perceptions of time. Studying them is one way to ponder the Jews' unique victimisation during the Second World War.

Endnotes

1. Adam Czerniakow, *The Warsaw Diary of Adam Czerniakow: Prelude to Doom*, ed. Raul Hilberg, Stanislaw Staron and Josef Kermisz, trans. Stanislaw Staron and the staff of Yad Vashem (New York: Stein and Day, 1979), 287.

2   Ida Fink, *A Scrap of Time and Other Stories*. trans. Madeline Levine and Francine Prose (New York: Pantheon Books, 1987), 3, 6. I am grateful to Debórah Dwork for drawing my attention to this book.

3   Gustav Biclfinger, *Die mittelalterichen Horen und die modernen Studen: Ein Beitrag zur Kulturgeschichte* (Stuttgart: W. Kohlhammer, 1892), 142.

4   Jacques Le Goff, *Pour un autre Moyen Age: temps, travail et culture en Occident* (Paris: Gallimard, 1977), Ch. 3.

5   Emmanuel Le Roy Ladurie, *Montaillou, village occitan de 1294 à 1324* (Paris: Gallimard, 1975), 419-31.

6   For attitudes in the Yishuv see Dina Porat, *The Blue and Yellow Stars of David: The Zionist Leadership in Palestine and the Holocaust, 1939-1945*. trans David Ben-Nahum (Cambridge, Mass.: Harvard University Press, 1990); Dalia Ofer, *Escaping the Holocaust: Illegal Immigration to the Land of Israel, 1939-1944* (New York: Oxford University Press, 1990); Tom Segev, *The Seventh Million: The Israelis and the Holocaust*. trans. Haim Watzman (New York: Hill and Wang, 1993), Parts I and H.

7   Leonard Baker, *Days of Sorrow and Pain: Leo Baeck and the Berlin Jews* (New York: Oxford University Press, 1978), 218.

8   H.R. Kedward, *In Search of the Maquis: Rural Resistance in Southern France* (Oxford: Clarendon Press, 1993), 73.

9   Marta Appel, unpublished memoirs, 1940-41, quoted in Monika Richarz, ed., *Jewish Life in Germany: Memoirs from Three Centuries.* trans Stella P. Rosenfeld and Sidney Rosenfeld (Bloomington, Indiana: Indiana University Press, 1991), 358.

10 Quoted in Lucy Dawidowicz, *A Holocaust Reader* (New York: Behrman House, 1976), 147, emphasis in original.

11 Yitzhak Arad, Yisrael Gutman and Abraham Margaliot, eds., *Documents on the Holocaust: Selected Sources on the Destruction of the Jews of Germany and Austria, Poland and the Soviet Union* (Jerusalem: Yad Vashem, 1981), 87-8

12 Emil Dorian, *The Quality of Witness: A Romanian Diary 1937-1944.* ed. Marguerite Dorian, trans. Mara Soceanu Vamos (Philadelphia: Jewish Publication Society of America, 1982), 38.

13 Stefan Zweig, *The World of Yesterday: An Autobiography* (Lincoln, Nebraska: University of Nebraska Press, 1964), 364. On the German-Jewish identity see George L. Mosse, *German Jews beyond Judaism* (Bloomington, Indiana: Indiana University Press, 1985).

14 Jean Améry, *At the Mind's Limits* trans. Sindey Rosenfeld and Stella P. Rosenfeld (New York: Schocken Books, 1986), 50.

15 Francis R. Nicosia, "The End of Emancipation and the Illusion of Preferential Treatment: German Zionism, 1933-1938," *Leo Baeck Institute Year Book XXXVI* (1991), 257; Abraham Margaliot, "The Reaction of the Jewish Public in Germany to the Nuremberg Laws," *Yad Vashem Studies.* XII (1977), 75-75-107.

16 E. Rosenbaum and A.J. Sherman, *Das Bankhaus M.M. Warburg & Co.* 1798-1938 (Hamburg: Hans Christians Verlag, 1976), 197-8.

17 Richarz, *Jewish Life.* 356.

18 David Silberklang, "Jewish Politics and Rescue: The Founding of the Council for German Jewry," *Holocaust and Genocide Studies* 7 (1993), 341.

19 Avraham Barkai, *From Boycott to Annihilation:The Economic Struggle of German Jews. 1933-1943*. trans. William Tempter (Hanover, New Hampshire: University Press of New England, 1989), 85-7, 141-2.

20 Zweig, *World of Yesterday* 391.

21 Rosenbaum and Sherman, *Bankhaus M.M. Warburg*, 212.

22 Peter M. Rutkoff and William B. Scott, "Letters to America: The Correspondence of Marc Bloch, 1940-41," *French Historical Studies*. XII (1981), 276-303.

23 Raymond-Raoul Lambert, *Carnet d'un témoin 1940-1943*. ed. Richard Cohen (Paris: Fayard, 1985), 85-6, 119, 131, 138, 196, 236.

24 Pierre Vidal-Naquet, "Présentation d'un document: le journal de Me Lucien Vidal-Naquet," *Annales. Economies, Sociétés, Civilisations*. 48 (1993), 540-1.

25 Edwin Landau, 'My Life before and after Hitler' (unpub. manuscript,1940), quoted in Monika Richarz, *Jewish Life in Germany*. 312.

26 Dan Vittorio Segrè, *Memoirs of a Fortunate Jew: An Italian Story* (Bethesda, Maryland: Adler & Adler, 1987), 50-1.

27 Joseph Walk, ed., *Das Sonderrecht für die Juden im NS-Staat: Eine Sammlung der gesetzlichen Massnahmen und Richtlinen — Inhalt und Bedeutung* (Heidelberg: C.F. Muller Juristischer Verlag, 1981), 303; Raul Hilberg, *The Destruction of the European Jews* (rev. edn., New York: Holmes & Meier, 1985), I, 151.

28 Quoted in Paul Fussell, Wartime: *Understanding Behavior in the Second World War* (New York: Oxford University Press, 1989), 76.

29 Jacques Biélinky, *Journal 1940-1942: Un journaliste juive à Paris sous l'Occupation* ed. Renée Poznanski (Paris: Editions du Cerf, 1992), 78-9, 86, 97, 110, 121, 142, 263.

30 Chaim Kaplan, *The Warsaw Diary of Chaim A. Kaplan trans* and ed. Abraham I. Katsh (New York: Collier, 1973), 45, 119.

31 Ibid, 206, 287, 342, 375; Joseph Kermish, ed., *To Live with Honor and Die with Honor: Selected Documents from the Warsaw Ghetto Underground Archives "O.S."* (Oneg Shabbath) (Jerusalem: Yad Vashem, 1986), 155.

32 See, for example, Czerniakow, *Warsaw Diary*. 86, 129, 132, 154, 191, 195, 205, 360-1, 364, 367, 373-5, 377-8, 380-1.

33 Francis Henry, *Victims and Neighbors: A Small Town in Nazi Germany Remembered* (South Hadley, Mass.: Bergen & Garvey, 1984), 85.

34 Anne Frank, *The Diary of a Young Girl* trans B.M. Mooyart-Doubleday (New York: Doubleday, 1953), 33.

35 *Ibid*, 67.

36 Janina Bauman, *Winter in the Morning: A Young Girl's Life in the Warsaw Ghetto and Beyond 1939-1945* (New York: Free Press, 1986), 140.

37 Carlo Levi, *Christ Stopped at Eboli: The Story of a Year*. trans, Frances Frenaye (New York: Farrar, Straus, 1963), 15.

38 Debórah Dwork, *Children with a Star: Jewish Youth in Nazi Europe* (New Haven, Conn.: Yale University Press, 1991), 74-5. See Avraham Seligmann, "An Illegal Way of Life in Nazi Germany," *Leo Baeck Institute Year Book XXXVII* (1992), 327-61.

39 Fink, *Scrap of Time*, 7-8

40 David Roskies, *Against the Apocalypse: Responses to Catastrophe in Modern Jewish Culture* (Cambridge, Mass.: Harvard University Press, 1984), 197.

41 Emmanuel Ringelblum, *Notes from the Warsaw Ghetto. The Journal of Emmanuel Ringelblum* ed. and trans. Jacob Sloan (New York: Schocken Books, 1974), 82, 300.

42 Quoted in Sarah Horowitz, "Voices from the Killing Ground," in Geoffrey H. Hartman, ed., *Holocaust Remembrance: The Shapes of Memory* (Oxford: Basil Blackwell, 1994), 50. See Dan Michman, "Jewish Religious Life under Nazi Domination: Nazi Attitudes and Jewish Problems," *Studies in Religion/Sciences religieuses* 22 (1993), 147-65.

43 Avraham Tory, *Surviving the Holocaust: The Kovno Ghetto Diary.* ed Martin Gilbert and Dina Porat, trans. Jerzy Michalowicz (Cambridge, Mass.: Harvard University Press, 1990), 253-6, 307-9, 492.

44 Ringelblum, *Notes from the Warsaw Ghetto.* 87

45 Abraham Lewin, *A Cup of Tears: A Diary of the Warsaw Ghetto.* ed. Anthony Polonsky, trans Christopher Hutton (Oxford: Basil Blackwell, 1988), 1304. Lewin attempted to survey Jewish opinion in the Warsaw Ghetto on this subject and concluded that the "lengtheners" were in a decisive majority." Ibid, 131.

46 Yitzhak Arad, *Ghetto in Flames: The Struggle and Destruction of the Jews in Vilna in the Holocaust* (Jerusalem: Yad Vashem, 1980), 343, 427.

47 Isaiah Trunk, *Judenrat, The Jewish Councils in Eastern Europe under Nazi Occupation* (New York: Macmillan, 1972), 423, 431-2.

48 Israel Gutman, *The Jews of Warsaw, 1939-1943-: Ghetto, Underground, Revolt* trans. Ina Friedman (Bloomington, Indiana: Indiana University Press, 1982), 84; Charles Roland, *Courage Under Siege: Starvation, Disease, and Death in the Warsaw Ghetto* (New York: Oxford University Press, 1992), 187.

49 Dwork, *Children with a Star* 180-1.

50 Yitskhok Rudashevski, *The Diary of the Vilna Ghetto, June 1941 - April 1943* (Israel: Ghetto Fighter's House and Hakibbutz Hameuchad, 1973), 56, 65, quoted in Dwork, *Children with a Star* 184.

51 Janina Bauman, *Winter in the Morning: A Young Girl's Life in the Warsaw Ghetto and Beyond 1939-1945* (New York: Free Press, 1986), 61.

52 Willy Lindwer, *The Last Seven Months of Anne Frank.* trans. AlisonMeersschaert (New York: Pantheon Books, 1991), 115-16.

53 Quoted in Roland, *Courage Under Siege* 196.

54 Lucjan Dobroszycki, ed., *The Chronicle of the Lodz Ghetto 1941-1944* trans. Richard Lourie, Joachim Neugroschel et al (New Haven, Conn.: Yale University Press, 1984), 65.

55 Tory, *Surviving the Holocaust* 87 n. 2.

56 *Ibid*, 116, 132, 229.

57 Trunk, *Judenrat* 91.

58 Kermish, *Selected Documents*, 65.

59 Kaplan, *Warsaw Diary* 244-5.

60 Bauman, *Winter in the Morning*, 61.

61 Fink, *Scrap of Time*. 31-4.

62 Yisrael Gutman and Daniel Blatman, "Youth and Resistance Movements in Historical Perspective," *Yad Vashem Studies*. XXIII (1993), 37.

63 Harold Werner, *Fighting Back: A Memoir of Jewish Resistance in World War II*. ed. Mark Werner (New York: Columbia University Press, 1992), 93, 111, 116.

64 Peter Silverman, David Schmusschkowitz and Peter Schmusschkowitz, *From Victims to Victors* (Toronto: n.d., [1992]), 136, 142.

65 Tory, *Surviving the Holocaust*. 306.

66 See Yitzhak Zuckerman ("Antek"), *A Surplus of Memory: Chronicle of the Warsaw Ghetto Uprising* trans and ed. Barbara Harshav (Berkeley, Calif.: University of California Press, 1993), 349, 374, 512; Gutman and Blatman, "Youth and Resistance Movements in Historical Perspective," 37.

67 Arad, *Ghetto in Flames* 417.

68 *Ibid* 478-80.

69 Zuckerman, *Surplus of Memory*, 336.

70 *Ibid*, 266, emphasis in original, 307.

71 *Ibid*, 314.

72 Arad, *Ghetto in Flames*. 480.

73 Ruth Rubin, *Voices of a People: The Story of the Yiddish Folksong* (2nd edn., New York: McGraw-Hill, 1973), 453-5. I am grateful to Hesh Troper for referring me to "Zog nit keynmol".

74 See the excellent discussion of "camp time" and "inmates' time" in Wolfgang Sofsky, *Die Ordnung des Terrors: das Konzentrationslager* (Frankfurt am Main: Fischer Verlag, 1993), chs. 7 and 8.

75 Primo Levi, *The Drowned and the Saved*. trans. Raymond Rosenthal (New York: Vintage Books, 1989), 76, 148. See Alvin Rosenfeld, "Jean Améry as Witness," in Hartman, *Holocaust Remembrance*, 59-69.

76 Jorge Semprun, *The Long Voyage*. trans. Richard Seaver (New York: Schocken Books, 1990), 203, 224.

77 Elie Cohen, *Human Behaviour in the Concentration Camp* trans. M.H. Braaksma (London: Free Association Books, 1988), 123.

78 Quoted in Lawrence Langer, "Remembering Survival," in Hartman, *Holocaust Remembrance* 78.

79 See Rudolf Vrba, *44070: The Conspiracy of the Twentieth Century* (Bellingham, Washington: Star & Cross, 1989), 226.

80 Tadeuz Borowski, *This Way to the Gas Ladies and Gentlemen,* (Harmondsworth, England: Penguin Books, ed. and trans. Barbara Vedder 1967), 131.

81 Robert-Jan Van Pelt, "A Site in Search of a Mission," in Yisrael Gutman and Michael Berenbaum, eds., *Anatomy of the Auschwitz Death Camp* (Bloomington, Indiana: Indiana University Press, 1994), 131-3.

82 Primo Levi, *Survival in Auschwitz* (New York: Collier Books, 1961), 107.

83 *Ibid*, 106.

84 Iris Murdoch, *The Black Prince* (London: Chatto & Windus, 1973), 248.

85 Sofsky, *Ordung des Terrors*. 93.

86 Cohen, *Human Behaviour in the Concentration Camp*, 128-9

87 Anna Pawelczynska, *Violence and Values in Auschwitz: A Sociological Analysis* trans. Catherine S. Leach (Berkeley, Calif.: University of California Press, 1979), 58.; Levi, Survival in Auschwitz 64, 85-6, 127, 155.

88 Borowski, *This Way to the Gas Ladies and Gentlemen* 132.

89 Nathan Cohen, "Diaries of the Sonderkomandos in Auschwitz: Coping with Fate and Reality," *Yad Vashem Studies* XX (1990), 273-312; Erich Kulka, *Escape from Auschwitz* (South Hadley, Mass.: Bergen & Garvey, 1986), 64.

90 Mary S. Costanza, *The Living Witness: Art in the Concentration Camps and Ghettos* (New York: Free Press, 1982), 61.

Insights into a Time and Place: Listen to These Women Survivors of the Nazi Camps Whose Character, Courage, Love and Hope, Beyond Good Luck, Overcame Hate

Leah Dickstein, M.D., Daniel P. Dickstein, M.D., and Steven G. Dickstein, M.D.

I am deeply honoured to have been invited by Sara Elkes, Director of the Elchanan Elkes Association for Inter-Community Understanding, to share my ongoing research in listening to and learning from women survivors of the Nazi camps. On Friday, December 1, 1995, by telephone from Florida Dr. Joel Elkes told me that his mother, Miriam, a Stutthof Germany camp survivor, used a comb fragment every morning to maintain her sense of self and kept a piece of bread with her in case someone needed it more than she. This work is entitled, "Insights Into a Time and Place: Listen to These Women Survivors of the Nazi Camps Whose Character, Courage, Love and Hope, Beyond Good Luck, Overcame Hate". To begin, I want to thank my sons, Drs Daniel and Steven, for their work since 1989, in Poland and Israel twice, and in the U.S., helping me conduct 104 interviews with women, and 100 thus far with men; my husband, Dr. Herbert Dickstein, for his emotional, technical and financial support; our Polish translators Wanda Waligora, Richa Zachariasz, and medical student, now physician, Dobromila Drop; my cousin Irwin's daughters Lisa and Judith Talesnick, Felice Kann Zisken and Iris Berlatzsky at Yad Vashem.

Before sharing what I have learned, it is important that you understand my involvement. Despite his efforts, my maternal grandfather Jake's youngest sister, Asneh Engelman, never came from Brest Litovsk i.e. Lithuania, with her husband and 3 sons to join her 2 older brothers, Jake and Arke, older sister, Bessie, and father, Solomon, in North America. As a small child in 1938-40, I recall my grandmother, Jake, speaking with my grandmother, Gussie, several times about sending money and packages; they did, then I saw no tears and heard no more.

In the mid 1950s I lived in Belgium and after 3 years, a Dutch Protestant neighbor introduced herself and told me about riding the trains at night to Holland to successfully hide her Latvian Jewish engineer husband with her brave and caring family. In the 1960s I met a French woman camp survivor in Israel who preferred not to speak about the war. In the mid 1970s I treated two men camp survivors and listened to one of their camp survivor wives describe their 3 year old daughter being ripped apart from her arms. Their living children knew, and still know, nothing of their war experiences and the survivor couple is dead. I have treated adult children of survivors and have been reading and thinking about that time for more than four decades. For three decades, I have been involved in women's and men's issues and studies; and, for more than two decades, I have treated patients with posttraumatic stress disorder of different etiologies.

In 1988 I invited Dr. Ignacy Wald, psychiatry professor at the Institute of Psychiatry in Warsaw, to speak at the American Psychiatric Association's Montreal meeting. When we met I told him my maternal grandparents emigrated from Brest-Litovsk, i.e. Lithuania in 1906. He said Brest was only a few hours east of Warsaw and I must come some day. The next winter he invited me to speak at the Polish Psychiatric Association's Psychotherapy meeting in Gydansk in May '89. I could not because of the APA meeting, so he wrote - "then when?" Daniel and I arrived in June 1989. I gave 2 lectures, had dinner at Dr. Wald's home and learned only in 1995 in Warsaw from his cousin, a woman who had been a hidden child survivor, that he, now dead, was also Jewish and a Nazi camp survivor!

In 1989, I learned that Dr. Anna Ornstein, a world renowned child psychoanalyst, was taken in 1944 at 17 from Hungary to Auschwitz and survived with her extraordinary mother and older cousin. She graciously consented to be our first interviewee at her Cincinnati home and connected me through her cousin Millie, to Wanda Waligura, a Catholic Warsaw journalist.

What I sought in a 13 page 103 item gender-specific questionnaire I would complete as I listened, was understanding women's unique thinking, feelings, competencies, capacities and incapacities for dealing with what were impossible circumstances. Dr. Ornstein stated, "the literature was too superficial, offered too many generalizations, and there was no place to recognize coping skills or the importance of hope." She said, "Survival was possible if you lived on two simultaneous levels: 1. don't cry or become depressed, pay close attention to what is going on, i.e. be hyper-alert, look O.K., lick every drop of available water and, simultaneously, 2. preserve your individual self; your past, talk about memories, your values, and create or maintain current caring relationships, like a family." She added: "The primary experience was hunger, and thirst; the first survival lesson: cooperation i.e. in crowded barracks taking turns with space to lean on someone's back or stretch one's legs," or sharing food. "Her parents had ensured that she developed a strong Jewish identity which she believes was a decisive factor in her ability to adapt to the extreme camp conditions and in living a healthy post-war life." In Auschwitz, after losing her name to a number and all her body's hair, she had to quickly pick two shoes whose fit would eventually mean life, or death if blisters became infected and were naturally untreated.

"Organizing" was an equally important skill i.e. stealing and finding things that could be usable: a scrap of food, a piece of string, a spoon, some water to wash in, a pencil stub, potato skins from the garbage pile. Organizing for oneself and one's close relationships, while not hurting another prisoner, was part of survival, like "'finding' a cabbage rolling off a wagon." Melinas, i.e. a hiding place in one's clothing, hidden clothing pockets, were made to store these treasures.

I learned from Dr. Ornstein that I was right to ask about pre-war lives because survivors brought them to camp. She was fortunate to sleep with her mother and cousin on a crowded bunk, their home. Creating and maintaining trusting, caring, loving relationships with commitment, sharing everything, sacrificing for others, displaying loyalty, and even having disagreements with a few women, meant survival. These relationships of non-family, begun in camp, continue to today. Dr. Ornstein recounted that receiving her tattoo on her second entrance to Auschwitz brought her hope that she would at least have another day. Her mother found an apple core walking back to camp after factory work and saved it for Anna's 18th birthday and her recovery from typhoid fever and time in the revier, i.e. hospital, where she fantasized about eating apples and tomatoes by biting and not slicing them. At liberation, as she reached for sugar in a ransacked storage area, separated from her mother in the pandemonium, she heard her mother scream, "Don't touch it. It could kill you." And she didn't.

Irena Gajewska started her interview in a new Warsaw coffeehouse on the main boulevard by confronting me with a question: "Why so late?" Why did someone come in 1989 to ask her about her experiences when she needed and wanted to speak after liberation and, instead, was given symptomatic anti-anxiety and sleeping pills for four decades. She was arrested returning from church and an underground (the A.K.) organization meeting. She felt foolish to have all the documents in her pocket wrapped in her handkerchief and discarded them on her way to prison with the police. She had drawn Fort BEM where the ammunition factory was and they questioned her overnight at Commisor #7 on Krochmal Street. Then she was taken to Gestapo headquarters, then to Warsaw's Pawiak prison and questioned roughly. Many Catholic women said their experiences in Pawiak were worse than in the camps. However, a prison translator tried to help her. He had lost a daughter her age and his Russian wife worked with her brother. After release from prison she hid, working in a hospital and continued her underground work until the Warsaw Uprising, when she was sent to Ravensbruck and then to Sachsenhausen. She was beaten mercilessly because she broke a boring machine in the leather factory. She declined to be a 'shtubowa', i.e. a room overseer of lower status. She was 23 and had studied economics. But the women prisoners voted for her because she could be trusted, especially with the most important task of equally dividing food, especially potatoes whose skins could look okay but whose insides could be rotten. They all knew each piece of bread or potato was really one human life. She closed her eyes when she divided the food to show she was fair. Once, walking from camp she "organized" i.e. picked up a nail from the road and in the factory found threads so she wove something and made underwear which they didn't get. She always had manual skills, repaired the wooden shoes and made a rosary from wood scraps. "It was a way to get away from camp by praying; she still has it." She saved pieces of bread and margarine every day, organized pencils and made a manger drawing for the wall on Christmas eve with the saved, now "Christmas" bread. Women came to sing songs and tried to get pieces of Christmas trees to remind themselves of home. They had planned this Christmas for several months. A woman painter prisoner painted Irena's portrait as a gift for the celebration, which she still treasures. Once she hemorrhaged from her gums so they extracted, i.e. dug out, all her teeth and she convulsed. She was taken to the revier where a nurse used two of her ten tampons to stop the bleeding; she was expected to die. However, she thought positively about how to survive the next minute. Her weight went from 63 to 33 kilograms from this episode. Although Polish prisoners could receive monthly packages, the guards stole much of them. She described how women had to strip to have all body hair cut; some were then selected by the SS for 'poof', i.e prostitute houses.

Rachel Katz, petite and 28, was also selected to be a blockelste for 200 girls who, she proudly stated, trusted her. Interviewed in Jerusalem from Hungary she was the only member of the Judenradt, i.e. Jewish Council in Debutzen, her home, who had the courage to speak German to the Germans. In camp she always confronted the German ouzier (guard) with, "Why do you beat the women?" "You don't have a mother?" The response was "You have too much chutzpah, i.e. nerve." Rachel retorted, "that's my nature. I tell it. I do what's good for you and the girls." She was beaten once for speaking up, to the point she forgot her telephone number and address. All one thousand of her girls came to her with problems. She had wanted to become a lawyer. They worked in Marbor munitions factory and every few weeks they made a show. She learned to help others from her father at age six when he would help poorer townspeople. At a selection Mengele sent her to the left, aloud she called him a fahflookta. (a curse) He took out his revolver but she ran. Mengele said she'd see her family in a half-hour in the smoke. She was last to get clothing and found just a blanket to wrap herself in. Mengele asked, "Are you sick? Open the blanket." She said, "I gave others the clothing." She was beaten swollen and got clothes. She cooked field weeds in water stating, "if it's good for animals, it's good for you." Some fasted on Yom Kippur, the Jewish Day of Atonement, others stole factory candles for Friday evening prayers. In her nightmares she still hears screaming of the night when the adjacent gypsy lager (barrack) of families were all taken to the crematoria. She escaped with 40 to the forest although all one thousand women on the Death March wanted to join her. She told the American liberators, "we need food not bubblegum." They gave her a car and driver. She was an interpreter to help catch Nazis and got the girls places to live, food and clothing in the nearby villages. With the car and driver, she went to Bergen Belsen and found her sister.

Isabella Marzec-Stvrna, a Cracow lawyer, first was sent to Cracow's Montelupe prison at 25, then to Ravensbruck because she was in the Underground. "Women were much stronger in camp, they don't collapse." "Hope" was the survivor's key. She "organized" newspapers, nails, joked with German guards, went to other blocks to tell women, "keep your hope up, don't suicide, the war will end." She felt no anxiety, was prepared to live or die, believed in fate. Once they stood for an appel (roll-call) for 60 hours without food, with dogs grabbing their clothes if they tried to sit.

Kamilla Janowicz-Svcz, interviewed in Warsaw, born in Brest Litovsk, like my maternal grandparents, at 19 was in the Cracow Underground as a scout, was caught and sent in 1941 to Lublin prison, then to Ravensbruck 48 miles north of Berlin. She refused "to allow them to kill her mind or take her soul." She unloaded bricks, sand, coal and building stones and was experimented on with typhus shots. Her family sent her one page a month of the book Pan Tadeuz hidden in bread to encourage her to live. She commented, "The flower of women intellectuals from the Underground were in camps." She still hasn't told her teacher-son much. She tied the camp gate closed with a string as she, nurse to those sicker, left, so it would never be opened again.

Wanda Marossany, found and interviewed in Warsaw, was in two prisons and then in Auschwitz where she noted "every day was different." Her entire Catholic family was in the Underground. They were allowed to write home in German once a month. She became depressed when her mother died in camp. Beaten by Ukrainian women, Jewish women took her to their barracks and fed her. Her great great grandmother was the first Polish pediatrician in the 1870s.

Susanna Weiss Brown, interviewed in Jerusalem, said her interview "is closing a circle for me, and was happy to speak," though she said, what many said, "for her, the Holocaust hasn't ended." In camp she was with her sister Aggie and could not have survived without her. She heard her mother shot, but had no time to mourn because she was busy with Aggie. She said, "women have more ability to suffer and know their responsibility was to survive." She did double work so her sister wouldn't be taken away. Until today she has no fear of people, only dogs. In camp women admired the sisters' relationship. "There wasn't an hour that passed that we didn't know what happen in the next hour." In camp she told Aggie "you can't leave me because we'll be together until 2001." They recited childhood novels; "suicide was a luxury I couldn't afford." Their childhood was happy and good. Their parents demonstrated the value of humanity and the meaning of life. As children, their mother took them to help out poor families. "Weakness, pessimism and suicide are against good," said mother. She was in the Auschwitz gas chambers and gas didn't come out. "From age 16, I had no elders in my life. The more horrors I saw, the stronger I became in order not to use oppression as the Germans did." She can't be in a closed room without windows or air; it reminds her of the gas chambers. She can't be without people. "I was busy with remaining alive: working, washing, eating, guarding each other and cleaning off lice."

Agnes (Aggie) Kreisler began with, "every day Auschwitz is on my mind." "Every piece of bread was tomorrow's life. Stutthof was the greatest shock: flowers, a lake, swans, and a few meters beyond, was the gas." Mother had told them, "Stay together and help each other." January 19, 1945 they got shots of strychnine or benzene in their arms. Susan, then 16, sipped it out from both of them. On the Death March, Susan was in better condition. Aggie's legs were frozen so she crawled on all fours two hundred meters at minus twenty degrees into the woods with Susan dragging her. Aggie was unconscious from being hit by a German on the left side of her neck and left for dead. Susan put leaves on the snow so she could retrace her steps to Aggie when she went to a village to find water. She returned and dragged Aggie to a barn for two days. Russian soldiers came and Susan yelled "We are here, come help us." Russians told Poles to help Aggie; they refused. So Susan carried Aggie to another village and Poles helped them saying, "Maybe our son in Russia will need help from people there." At age 20 Aggie's legs were amputated, without narcotics, because of gangrene, by medic-soldiers. Drunken Russian soldiers abused Susan and took them to Tambov in Russia for more surgery. Susan worked as a nurse on the venereal disease ward in exchange. After several months, Susan took Aggie home by train on a stretcher and watched her constantly so she wouldn't suicide. She finally got prostheses and they emigrated to Israel, after Susan attended photography school in Prague and Aggie ran a perfumery and photo shop. Aggie has worked continuously since her second day of arrival in Israel, including encouraging the wounded to live. Susan had told her she couldn't die because they had no burial shroud.

Eulalia Rudak in 1989 was vice president of the Warsaw City Association of Fighters and Invalids of Polish Wars since 1918. At 12 she was sent to Auschwitz-Birkenau because she, a Catholic, was an underground scout. In camp German soldiers examined naked women vaginally with sticks and lamps looking for jewellery and coins. She was beaten, starved for days, met an aunt who pretended to be her mother to protect her. As a child in camp she received only a cup, not a bowl, of soup. They were overrun with lice and spent hours picking them off their bodies and clothing. She didn't suicide because she had her aunt. Mengele took her to his room, tried to rape her; she screamed and ran. After she stole leftovers from the kitchen where she cooked for German soldiers, they retaliated by firing guns with rock salt behind her knees. She "organized" anything she could find. She got margarine on a tiny coffeespoon because she worked in a factory. Sometimes women stole bread and shoes from each other. With diarrhea, the women owsiers used a floor brush and spread excrement on the children's bread. She was a stube woman chosen by her peers because she was honest and fair. They voted with tree leaves and paper. She still likes to help women. She didn't cry until she was liberated on May 1, 1945 and has spoken to schoolchildren since 1970.

Maria Borowska-Baver began by saying "Auschwitz was my place to be as a Polish woman, with a Jewish father." Her first husband, Tadeuz Borowski wrote, *This Way For the Gas Ladies and Gentlemen*. Maria served in the Underground at the University, was sent to prison and then to Auschwitz. She had wanted to be a teacher, but after the war, felt she had nothing to tell the young and became a journalist. Her then fiance Borowski would organize cigarettes and medicine for her when he came to work fixing something in her camp. She believed men were better organized in camp. Friendship kept her alive. In 1951 her only child, a daughter, was born and she developed insomnia with the nightmare that the Germans came and put her child in the ovens. Three days after the child was born, her husband comitted suicide.

Wanda Stvrczula, interviewed in Poland, an athlete and underground scout, helped raise children and completed medical school after the war and became a paediatrician. "In camp the young helped the old." She was injected in her ovaries and uterus. However, she bore a son and daughter later. In camp she developed skin blisters from avitaminosis. She found a book, *How to Imitate Christ*, which they were to burn, but she kept hidden. She learned French in camp from a girl and found a photo of a group of boys; one was her brother. She worked in 'Canada', the barrack which contained all the prisoners' belongings.

Trudi Simon Berger, interviewed in Jerusalem, still takes a tranquilliser in order to sleep. She is an optimist like her father; in camp she lived to protect her mother. She had self-confidence and promised herself in camp, if she survived, she would help poor children because she was raised as a spoiled child; she has. In Israel she led the adoption of 50 families forty years ago by a group of women. She also began free dental clinics for children. As a woman she had an indomitable spirit though she had no childhood. "It feels like yesterday crossing the bridge into the Kovno Ghetto". She worked in the Ghetto hospital and was saved from the Lithuanians by their family maid. In the hospital she met Axel Benz, a German soldier of the Mercedes Benz Company. He gave her his gold watch to trade for food. She got jam, bread and butter, was caught and beaten. On the train to Stutthof at sixteen and a half she wanted to jump because the guards fell asleep, but her forty-two year old mother, who looked sixty-two, couldn't. So she stayed with her mother. She was called a wonder child because she always had survival ideas. "I became my mother's mother." Her mother tried to deny Trudi as her daughter to protect her, but Trudi gave her blue skirt and red blouse to her mother, wore her mother's black dress, adding saliva to mother's cheeks for colour so her mother wouldn't be selected to be killed. She dug ditches and accidentally stuck a shovel in her foot which became gangrenous. She was sent to the crematorium but the gas wasn't working and then survived in the last second before being pushed into the oven. She was taken to the revier and treated by Dr. Kaplanita, a Kovno surgeon. As the Russians approached, the Germans sent the women to the boats. She and mother were on a pig boat with straw for 13 days without food. They drank seawater and the straw began to burn as the English bombed the boats near Kiel. Of three hundred women on this boat, only thirty remained. Trudi carried her mother on her back out of the hold despite her painful foot. The captain gave her his bloody blanket and died. Polish and German guards screamed at the women to jump into the water. She lay on top of her mother and saved her. She believes you must help yourself and others, not forget, but somehow forgive. Axel found her afterwards, wanted to marry her and go to Israel; she said, "I can't."

Hanni Kolumbus-Krisoin, interviewed in Jerusalem, worked as a volunteer in the Kovno small ghetto orphanage, had wanted to become a physician and was home sick one day when the orphanage was deported. Mother was 44; Hanni, at age 20, put her 10 people ahead in the selection so she would follow the way her mother was sent. The first day in Stutthof a German soldier said "you can shine my shoes for extra bread and cheese." She, "I have never shined shoes for a German and I won't." She was transferred to the worst sub-camp, Malkin, and dug ditches 3 meters deep for tanks. Mother peeled potatoes. She and her mother had no shoes; their feet had wounds so she requested to return with mother to Stutthof on the sick train. The German guards were drunk; the crematoria weren't working. An old classmate took her to the revier, washed and bandaged her legs; then the British bombed it. Mrs. Miriam Elkes was in the hospital too, with others to care for her. In February '45 the decree was the Death March, if you can walk in snow at minus 20 degrees centigrade day and night, or the crematoria. Hanni hid on the top bunk to stay with her mother. Germans came with dogs and didn't find her. One day they walked to the train and to the boats near Kiel and Hamburg. She and mother went on the barge. Planes came and there was much commotion. Hanni took Mrs. Elkes to Munich later with Mrs. Elkes' niece, via the Red Cross and to Santo Telya. Although their ship burnt, they were O.K. because it was an iron barge. Hanni spoke German and some German sailors helped her mother. They walked and took the train to Bergen Belsen. She and her friend Gita shared everything. They shared a fur jacket as they stood guard at night while the German woman kapo and her lover were together, and so got extra cheese and bread she gave to her mother. As a child in Memel she did gymnastics which made her healthy; she still does gymnastics twice a week. She had a sense of humour in camp. Her mother knew Chagall in Vitebsk, was well educated and lived with Hanni until age 83 in 1983; Hanni is proud of that. She is the only Israeli Board Member of the European Soroptimists.

Zofia Kann-Pocilowska, interviewed in Warsaw, was 21 when, as an 'underground' University courier between Lublin and Warsaw, she was arrested in March '41 from her Warsaw hiding place because someone arrested earlier had a membership list of the couriers. After a few days in Pawiak prison and in Lublin's Castle Gestapo prison, she was shipped to Ravensbruck. In 1943 she was in the revier 'prepped' to be experimented on the next day, but was returned to her block and participated in an organized protest with 50 already and 5 to be experimented upon women. One of the 50 women spoke German and told the German woman commandant, Langefeld, they refused to be guinea pigs and were prepared for a reprisal. She learned they were planning to transplant skin cancer from German women to these prisoners. Later in Langefeld's trial at Nurenberg, Zofia testified. In camp she carried and pushed stones, built roads, helped transport food and cut logs in the forests. Now she sculpts from logs. She was in the Ravensbruck camp Underground as a courier again carrying news, medicines, books and communion crackers from Polish soldier-prisoners into Ravensbruck camp. She and several women thought about escaping; these soldiers gave them a map, but they didn't escape because there were so many guards. She stole food from German guards. She participated in hidden classes because many political prisoners were university professors. She had spotted typhus in prison and twice again in camp. Nurses tried to distribute medicine which was controlled by the Germans. Her illegal camp occupation was drawing, which she had studied before. She learned to sculpt on her toothbrush with a little knife from a man soldier-prisoner. She made Christ on the Cross and sent it to her mother via the Underground to tell her mother she was alive. She also made many for ill friends in camp. Her interest in and career as a sculptor began in camp and continues today. After the war she studied at the Warsaw Academy of Arts. In camp others wrote and recited poetry. Everyone was depressed at times and felt broken, but they were in an atmosphere of mobilization; all depended on the state of their psyche, i.e. their positive attitude and mental state. She was prepared for the day she might die and planned to suicide if experimented on. Occasionally they received beet marmalade and only potato skins. She prayed in the beginning but stopped after she saw the hell around her. Her group of women wanted to survive; against the humiliation they wanted to keep face. During the long hours of roll call i.e. appell, one woman talked covertly about astronomy. She has carefully chosen what she tells her daughters. Although this interview took place in July 1989, when we visited Zofia again in June '95, her young adult granddaughter was with her and sadly told us her grandmother has never told her anything about her wartime, though Zofia told us earlier she had. During camp beatings they broke her glasses; she is nearly blind despite surgeries but continues to try to sculpt. She believed "in the end the bad couldn't win, so human beings must survive all the trauma". She would never think of killing someone despite all these experiences; she thinks men were more aggressive and the trauma made them more so. She is afraid of crowds and showed startled responses several times. She has created art work about the Holocaust and has had exhibits of this work.

Klara Landau Bondy, in Jerusalem, said, "optimism kept her alive and dance helps." At 23 she was with her sister and felt "you couldn't stay alive alone." The Nazis told her to dance and gave her a pajama-like costume to wear. She was so weak she fell down as she tried to stand up and dance, but she did dance. Onions were the only vitamin she received. The soup and/or "fake" coffee had bromine to tranquillise her. She washed her hair in tea because it was important to be clean, and exchanged 20 cigarettes for bread or margarine. She noted "women were made of gentle steel." She believed the women began new lives after the Death March from Auschwitz which was the worst experience, while men, she believes, are much different, "they lost themselves; many suicided". She has complete recall of all details including getting "organized" food from prisoners and, even once, a light blue brassiere and panties. One day she "bought" herself a broken piece of mirror to see herself. Until her retirement she has been a dance teacher as were her grandfather and father.

Shulamit Kaliff, interviewed in Jerusalem, was taken to camp at 14 from a Berlin orphanage. Her parents had divorced, her mother was in England. She believed it was much more important to have someone, not to be alone, and to give and to get help; "a person was more important than food." She was with her sister and several girls. Shulamit went with her guardian to Terezin in May '43 and to Auschwitz in September '43, with 18 to 20 year old women. Someone put a long coat on her to make her look older and she lived. A German woman officer, Mandel, remembered Alma Rose, Gustav Mahler's niece, from a Viennese concert, and so took her out of Mengele's experimental block 12 to be the camp orchestra conductor. Shulamit played the flute, (i.e. a recorder), in the orchestra, which she had learned in school. The 29 women in the orchestra were spoken to differently and in German. During the day they played in the block, and in the morning and evenings played at the gate, as prisoners left and returned from work. So she was busy 12 hours a day. Before being selected for the orchestra, she cried constantly. Every Sunday they gave a concert outside for the women prisoners. The SS came to their block and asked them to play, though not Wagner. She was once awakened at 2.00 a.m. to play, and at first thought they were going to the crematoria, but they had to play at 2.00 a.m. for the transport from Hungary, in April '44. Alma Rose often stood at the barracks door watching crematoria-flames; they never expected to survive. She feels those who haven't been in concentration camp can't interpret or measure the feelings and reactions of those who have. She didn't believe she'd survive, but had a strong will to. She said, "you can't know the power and strength to go on. "Just think about music, not about what you saw around you; use denial." She concluded, "I have only told you 1% of what I wanted to tell." "How do you explain the SS wanting to hear music, and the same men coming with dogs to kill prisoners." She couldn't be with normal people after liberation. Her mother found her and wanted to take her to England, but she needed to be with her "family" from camp. She commented, "what languages of emotions could I use with others who hadn't been in camp?"

She was sent later to Bergen Belsen with her sister and the orchestra, and changed her name. They came to Israel, and after her children were grown she earned a masters degree in biochemistry without completing high school. She agreed that women have more power to suffer, and more will to live and to bear and raise children. Survival depended on attitude. Though more women were murdered on arrival, more survived than men. She feels as though she's telling someone else's story.

Esther Lurie at 31 was sent to Stutthof in July '44 from the Kovno ghetto. German soldiers took her to draw portraits of their children, families, lovers. One German's girlfriend brought Esther onions as thanks; she shared them with the sick. A German guard she had drawn for sent her a cup of soup every day; she shared it. In winter she received a pair of socks for her drawing and gave them to her cousin. Taken to German homes from the ghetto to draw, she was given a meal, a whole bread was the best pay; she would trade away cigarettes. Some of the Germans said they were ashamed to guard women. "We stole all the time" and "Stutthof 's horror was offset a bit by drawing for capos for bread." She had a belief "We would survive", and told all women that repeatedly. The commandant arranged for an art studio for her in the ghetto, where she also hid children, and he came to discuss art. Avrom Tory, Dr. Elkes' secretary, saved her drawings with a priest.

She wrote a 300 page diary. She drew more aesthetic than tragic scenes in the ghetto. She commented, "Many survivors still feel hurt, humiliated, harmed, because they were disbelieved so didn't want to speak". She didn't tell her children, because she didn't want them growing up in such an atmosphere, but travelled to U.S. universities with her paintings to talk about the Holocaust. "This is our escape, that we can't, and won't believe it happened." She believes strongly that "Remembrance is the secret of redemption." At Nazi War trials her paintings were used as living evidence and testimony. A camp nurse saved the cotton wrapping from bandages so Esther could draw. She regarded her art as her duty to record. Sketching was dangerous in the ghetto streets, so some people acted as sentinels, to warn her when Germans were coming. She had returned from Palestine to Kovno because her sister needed her and was trapped there. She had studied art all through school and later in Belgium, graduating with greatest distinction from the Institute Superior des Arts Decoratif. In 1940 she painted a four by four meter portrait of Stalin for the Kovno theater. She continued her lifelong pattern in camp, when she could, of surmounting difficulties, step by step. In the ghetto she was asked to draw life out the window of the eltestenrat by the Jewish leaders. Through Avrom Tory, she met Professor Nachman Shapiro, who told her where to go to draw. 200 of her paintings were photographed and buried in pottery water jugs she asked the pottery workshop where she worked, to make. Since 1989 she has received more of her hidden paintings from a Lithuanian woman artist friend, who feared sending them until communism was overthrown. Women in the camp gave her paper and pencil stubs. She felt it her duty to create and thus be a living witness. She didn't draw from 1948 until the '67 war in Israel. She was liberated by the Red Army in the forest where they had been left by the retreating Germans. She knew Russian and had a British passport. She didn't want to talk though realized she had to tell. She added, "it becomes holy; telling must go on."

In Stutthof she held little pictures of people, i.e. of women, in her pocket, which she had drawn with splinters of wood, ink, and later, a pen and pencil. She took them, when she took a real shower, to guard them. She feels she owes something to those who died so doesn't say 'no' when people call, come, ask. After the war she painted no more people, only nature, with which she feels at ease.

Helen Waterford, interviewed in Chula Vista, California, in her thirties learned to discipline her thoughts in Auschwitz. Creating recipes helped her go to sleep at night. Her postwar plan was to find her hidden child in Holland; she did, and then to run a guest house. In camp Sunday afternoons were conversation times. People didn't want to listen for more than five minutes after the war. She lectured at universities across North America, with a former Nazi youth leader, and wrote her testimony, *Lily of the Valley*.

Interviewed in New Jersey, Esther Raab at 17 was shipped to, and later escaped from Sobibor, after a dream of her mother, who told her to go to a certain barn. She walked for two weeks at night in seeming circles, and came to the barn, where a white apparition flew from the loft. It was her brother who had had the same dream several weeks earlier and had been in the barn for a while.

Interviewed in Massachusetts Dr. Vera Laska from age 13, was in the Catholic Czech Underground, and smuggled people across the Czech-Hungarian border. She was scared all the time. Jan Mazerik was her humanitarian role model; "God was on vacation in camp." She learned fast not to stand out, but to live to tell. "Women knew when to be quiet and didn't react when slapped, but they talked a lot, wrote and composed in their minds and committed it to memory". They taught each other about plays, opera, poetry, songs and English. After the war she studied American history at the University of Chicago, planning to return to teach at Prague's Charles University. She married an American student and never did. She is professor at Boston's Regis College and has written a book about women survivors, realizing that is more important than her original area of scholarship.

Interviewed in Los Angeles, Ebi Gabor was liberated at 17 with her mother from Auschwitz, where she carried rocks. Every night in the bunks her mother said, "now we will cook with words." Her mother pleaded with her "do not go on the wire" i.e. don't suicide. She came from an outgoing, loving family; thought "Food, God and Hope." She was not a worrier; "It won't help." Her attorney son, now living next door, asked her to write; he had not read her book, *The Blood Tattoo.* as late as the early 1990s.

Interviewed in Louisville, Kentucky, Dr. Edith Eva Eger's best revenge to Hitler was her first grandchild. She wrote her doctoral thesis in the U.S. on, "Coping and Growth: A Theoretical and Empirical Study of Groups Under Moderate to Severe Stress". She wanted to be a dancer before her interrupted childhood. She was with her sister. She danced for Mengele, once came close to being raped by him in his office; the phone rang and she ran. They took her blood twice a week for the wounded German soldiers. She saw the additives used to drug them and stop their menstrual cycles floating as a thin skin on the weak, so-called "soup." "Jokes, i.e. gallows humour, were a way to interact, develop solidarity and relieve inner tensions." For example, "Did you know Hitler will die on a holiday? Certainly. Any day Hitler dies will be a holiday." For fun once they held a breast contest: i.e. breast shape and size. Food was the prize~ one prize for the young and one for the middle-aged. "I slept on my side, alternating head to foot so 6 of us could fit on a bunk 4 to 5 feet wide." "If I wanted to turn, I said so and we all counted, "1, 2, 3 turn." One could go to the latrine only when guards said O.K.; usually in the morning and at night where we "talked and heard rumours". She believes attitude and belief in the convergence of body, mind and spirit are most important, and women had more perseverance. She had an intense curiosity and desire to experience life and love and hung on fiercely to survive. At the end she chose one blade of grass over another to eat. "Rigidity led to death."

Interviewed in Margate, Florida, Rose Kleinman Steg, my father's neighbour, worked in Bjezinku camp sorting luggage and found babies in the luggage. When she told capos, she was beaten. She gave food away and threw gold into the latrines, fearful to hide it. Her 4 year old son and 6 year old daughter were murdered; they had "gone to the left" with her aunt. She'd worked on a farm before the war; she and her husband survived.

Interviewed in Jerusalem, Nitza Ganor at 18 wanted to live one hour more than Hitler.

Interviewed in Jerusalem, Edith Grunwald at 17, as a camp ouzier's maid, trained the ouzier's dog to eat her food so Edith could eat the better dog food. She shared everything, sure she'd return, wanting to be able to hold her head high.

Interviewed in Jerusalem, Fraydel (meaning joy) Lichtenstein, now Rena Quint, was born in Protrokov, Poland in December, 1935. An uncle told her, at 4, to run home to her father and she did, under a Gestapo man's legs from the synagogue roundup. He hid her disguised as a boy; both worked in a glass factory until a roundup in '43-'44 when they were shipped to Bergen Belsen. She travelled with a woman schoolteacher who pretended to be her mother, as nameless women continued to do until liberation. In the women's barracks, she was on the side with women with their children, not on the orphan side. She recalled "fences of dead bodies" and hearing women crack lice. She licked empty milk cans. She has 2 knee scars from dog bites. At liberation she had typhus and was taken to Sweden by a woman with her dead daughter's passport. She was adopted by a New York childless couple, is a Jerusalem Yad Vashem Museum guide and began speaking after 1981 when her third child, a son, told his teacher his mother was a survivor. The teacher didn't believe him, but asked her and she said 'yes', she was a survivor.

I have listened, with translators and without, and now you have listened through me, to these Catholic and Jewish women Nazi camp survivors share memories, with attention to detail, more vivid now with time. I have listened with translators and without in Polish, English, German, Russian, French, Spanish, Dutch, Hebrew and Yiddish, to women who, despite varying degrees of post-traumatic stress disorder and post-traumaic stress reaction, unnamed after the war, which impacted on their personal lives, have lived beyond survival, to make outstanding contributions to their worlds, in memory of those they lost through hate. After the war no one wanted to listen. Now these aging, intelligent, strong, hyper-alert, quick thinking, risk-taking, courageous women who maintained hope, who cared for and fed others' minds, bodies and spirits, at times, more than for themselves, with heavy hearts, sadness, pride and humility, want us to know as much as we can, for not having been there. These women, sex role socialized to assume women's stereotypic roles, displayed unexpected courage, strengths, will and determination and physical and psychological behaviours to survive, beyond the average of 5 weeks, while simultaneously maintaining their strong family and relational bonds. Mostly young, they lost their childhoods, adolescence, and prematurely matured to endure suffering and abuse, maintaining their sense of identity and self-worth. Most came from emotionally close and mentally healthy families. They took advantage of luck, talked, created, shared, encouraged, worked twelve hours a day, in addition to walking miles to and from the work sites: they dug trenches, built military fortifications, manufactured army supplies, built airports, dug in mines, repaired and built railroads, worked on farms, loaded and unloaded freight from trains and tugboats, operated electric power stations, cooked, did laundry, cleaned, loaded and unloaded cement, bricks and stones, sewed, made and repaired shoes. They had stamina, fantasized a future, didn't personalize the situation, took humiliation more readily and easily than men.

The survivor syndrome includes anhedonia, difficulty concentrating, anxiety, guilt feelings about surviving, hypermnesia for Holocaust events, fatigue, depression (episodic major depression and chronic dysthymia), emotional instability, psychosomatic disturbances, headaches, nightmares with Holocaust content, sleep disturbances and nervousness. I also found alienation of being and always remaining somehow "different", excessive eating problems, smoking, no sharing of their past with their children, even with spouses at times, over-protectiveness toward their children, including communicating to the children that the children must be all to the survivors because the survivors lost so much: parents, siblings, their planned futures: work and relationships and dreams. Yet lifelong emotional disability does not automatically follow early trauma. I hope and believe my listening has helped the survivors cope a bit better with their traumas and to live with more peace within themselves and with others.

They are surprised we want to know, even now. They are pleased to share and to realize that their indescribable suffering can be described and is of value, at least to professionals who make time to listen. They seem a bit more relaxed, less alienated, more self-accepting afterwards, more attached with a recognized, legitimate place in their current worlds.

In conclusion, history is of people's lives. These women are role models we all need across our lifetimes, whether we are women or men, regardless of our circumstances of gender, race, faith, age, socioeconomic, educational or political category.

On November 27, 1995, I received the postcard Minka Engelman sent on May 14, 1940 from Lomazy, Poland to her father, my great great

Uncle Moishe in New York. Stamped with the Swastika, written in German, she asked why she hadn't heard from him. She wrote repeatedly "we are O.K." I never knew about Minka until a month ago; her brother, Harry, a social worker and judge, who sent it to me, never spoke about her, nor did his father or his sister Anna in Brooklyn. There are no pictures. A friend told him a year ago he saw Minka, her 3 daughters, husband and father-in-law standing next to the ditch they dug outside of town, shot in the back of their heads, and fall in. There are no names or photos of these children, or of Minka. They did not have luck to be shipped to a Nazi camp. To their memories, and to the memories of the other millions similarly mistreated and murdered, we have dedicated this work!

112

Jewish Leadership Groups Under Nazi Occupation

Yehuda Bauer

Why did we choose this subject for tonight? It is not only because of the memory of Dr. Elchanan Elkes of the Kovno ghetto. It is also because it is of vital importance to study the behaviour of the victim community during genocide. We live in an age of genocide. The Holocaust was the extreme example of that, and it is very important first of all for the Jews to know how the Jewish leadership behaved, how it fared, what options it had, but it is also important for the general communities everywhere in the world, because victims of genocide are usually left behind. What many historians deal with is the perpetrator. We should address the reaction of victims and the reactions of the bystanders - those are topics that must be dealt with because we want to know how humans behave in extreme situations. What do they do? And so this kind of a general lecture tonight, which does not deal with any one particular Jewish council, but with the phenomenon of Jewish councils and maybe, if I have the time, a few other groups that were not the official leadership but the secondary leadership - that is something that has to be dealt with.

The problem in research is that most people who deal with Jewish reactions during the Holocaust do not compare Jewish reactions with non-Jewish reactions under Nazi rule. No comparison is made usually with what French mayors of cities did under German occupation, or Dutch, Polish, Czech mayors and so on. There is a vast difference of course between the fate of these peoples and the Jews because no-one but the Jew was slated for total and absolute murder of every single individual. But that they could not know when it started. So in 1940, 1941 and 1942, how did these local non-Jewish leadership groups behave?

There are two basic attitudes to the question of Jewish leadership in the historical literature. One is that by my friend and colleague Raul Hilberg who wrote his tremendously important study, *The Destruction of the European Jews*, which was published in Chicago, in 1961 - so that is quite a long time ago by now - and in subsequent articles and speeches he concentrates his attitude, or his analysis of the Jewish leadership in a chapter that he wrote in the volume *The Holocaust as a Historical Experience*, which was published by Holmes & Meyer in New York. In that chapter, what Hilberg says is this - The Nazis wanted to save manpower and money and effort, and so they tried to rule the Jewish communities through Jews, and because they exercised absolute terror against the Jewish populations, what they wanted to do was to include the Jewish leadership in their bureaucratic machinery. And they succeeded. Any Jewish leadership under the Nazis,- and the Nazis after 1939, after the conquest of Poland, called these leadership groups either Jewish councils or councils of Jewish elders, or some similar name - all these Jewish councils, Hilberg says, were part of the murder machinery. They were part of the Nazi bureaucracy, part of the Nazi plan to murder all the Jews. Jews were responsible, not because they wanted it, but because they were put into that situation by the Germans, for leading their communities into the slaughter. This is not a value judgement, Hilberg says, they had no choice. They did not know to start with that that would be the German plan, and it has no bearing on the personal worth of the individuals concerned. Objectively speaking, Hilberg says, they were part of the German bureaucratic machinery.

Now the other point of view was put forward first by a historian working at Yad Vashem, Aaron Weiss, in two major articles that were published very close in time to that book that I just mentioned, and then taken up by a number of historians including myself, and our response to Hilberg is this. Yes, you are right. Objectively speaking, the Jews who accepted, whether by force or by some other means, leadership positions in Jewish communities, were part of the machinery that the Germans intended to put into place in order to do whatever the German policy towards the Jews was. At first, until mid-1941 let us say, the Germans had not decided on the total murder of the Jews, so there were other plans, and then from that point on their policy was murder. However, it is not only the result that matters. Because if you want to know what happened to the Jewish communities, you do not need any research. You know that they were murdered. What is important is the intention, the intent of those leadership groups. What did they want to achieve? Not only what they failed to achieve, but what they wanted to achieve, and how they went about it. And when you examine intent or intention, you find that there are tremendous differences between the different Jewish councils all over Europe. In fact no two Jewish councils behaved in exactly the same way.

Each Jewish council presided over a hell, but the hells were different, although the result was the same in most places though not in all. And so the way that these people acted, how they did it, is as important as the result. Now how did these Jewish leadership groups come into existence? It started of course with the Jews in Germany. I think it is important in front of a public, part of which is Jewish and part of which is not Jewish, to emphasise that there were very few places in the world prior to 1933 where the Jews formed a united community in the modern world. One of the interesting exceptions is Great Britain where the Board of Deputies of British Jews has existed for the last 220 years or so, not that every Jew today in Britain has, or pays, allegiance to the Board of Deputies. So Britain also today has fallen into the same kind of structure that other Jewish communities have. But there was never any united Jewish community in Germany. There were Jewish communities in Baden and in Hessen and in Prussia and in Bavaria and in Hanover, and so on, prior to 1933, but there was never a united Jewish community in Germany. There was an official one in France, but most Jews did not belong to it. There was no united Jewish community, certainly not in Poland. In Hungary the Austro-Hungarian Empire tried to set one up and it split apart as it always does, because no two Jews can ever agree on anything! So you see the image that the Nazi had of Jews, of this world-wide Jewish conspiracy, is a contradiction in terms. There can be no Jewish conspiracy by definition. Had there been one there would not have been a Holocaust. So Jewish communities were always split.

Now in Germany, in the face of this danger of the Nazi take-over, attempts were made as early as 1932 which failed, and then there was another attempt that was made in April 1933, just after Hitler came to power, which failed. Jews could not unite, and only in September 1933 the *Reichsvetretung*, the 'Representation of Jews in Germany' came into being. Not every Jewish group belonged to it. Not until 1938 did everyone belong. But it came into being as a result of Jewish initiative, not of Nazi pressure. The Nazis could not have cared less. The Jews felt that they needed to have some kind of a body that represented them, that could defend them, that could look after social welfare, after education, after health, after emigration. And a political representation - you see the peculiar thing was that the Nazis abolished all political parties, of course. The only political group that was not Nazi in Germany was this Representation of Jews, because they were not Germans, so they could have representation under Nazi rule. They were the enemy. As a result, the Nazis accepted that the Jews should have a representation, though they did not recognise it legally. The only newspapers, two at first and then one, that were not under immediate Nazi control were Jewish - because they were not published by Germans they were all right. When the Nazis strengthened their hold over the Jewish life in Germany they more and more pressured the representatives of the Jews into a kind of stranglehold from which these people could not escape any more. The behaviour of these German Jews is quite contrary to the image that most people have. They were very courageous. They stood up to the Nazis, and they paid for it, most of them.

In 1939, after the so-called Kristalnacht pogrom, when the Jewish representation was dissolved by the Nazis, they re-established it under a new name, *Reichvereinigung*, and that representation was charged with emigrating as many Jews as possible. The leaders of those groups had every possibility of escaping from Germany, and they took the decision, with one or two exceptions, to stay until the last Jew left. That was an illusion of course. They could not know that. The leaders smuggled out, or officially emigrated out, most of the families -wives, children. In April 1941, a year and a half after the beginning of the war, the leaders of the German and Austrian Jewish communities were invited by the American Jewish Joint Distribution Committee, the main support group of American Jews for European Jewry, to Lisbon to discuss emigration. April 1941! And the Nazis permitted them to go. They had their families outside already, and the leaders of the JDC told them 'why do not you stay out?' 'No, we're going back. We have a responsibility to our communities.' And they returned, with one exception. The image that one has of this obedient German Jewish group is quite wrong. Of course they failed. They failed to emigrate after they realised the danger after 1938. They tried to emigrate people and failed. When they were told by the Nazis that they would all be deported to Madagascar, which was going to be the solution to the Jewish problem, all European Jews were to go to Madagascar, in 1940, they opposed it, but it did not help them much. Two at least of the leaders were arrested and put into concentration camps. None survived.

When the Nazis occupied Poland they had not the slightest idea what to do with the Jews. There was no plan. It is quite mistaken to think that the Nazis had a plan. It was only three weeks after the beginning of the war, on 21 September 1939, that a meeting of high SS officers in Berlin decided, on explicit instructions from Adolph Hitler himself, what to do with the Jews in Poland, to put them near railway lines so that they could be deported and thrown into Soviet Russia - all the millions of Jews of Poland and Germany and Austria and Bohemia and Moravia (which were then under German control), and to establish Jewish councils - the councils that I spoke about. Yes, the German example, but differently. The Jewish council would have to obey every order - that's what they were there for - and if there was any kind of objection they would be dealt with harshly. The Jews did not have any inkling, of course, of that meeting or those decisions. From the Jewish point of view this was a terrible new power in Poland with which they did not know how to deal. They had no preparation for it. They did not know what the Nazis were going to do, and in many places - not in every place - the leadership, the Jewish council, was elected or appointed by the Jews and then approved by the Germans.

In Warsaw the leadership of Jews was appointed by the last Polish mayor when the city was under siege by the Germans. The leader's name was Adam Czerniakow, and he was appointed by the Poles before they surrendered, and when the Germans marched into Warsaw there was a Jewish committee there, and that became the Judenrat. In Lublin there was fear about what to do. Nobody wanted to be in the Judenrat. In the end there was a decision that the responsibility to the community demanded that the people who had been officials of the Jewish community before the war should coalesce from wall to wall, from left to right, from religious and non-religious, and set up a committee, and that committee became the council of elders of Lublin. In Czestochowa, which is a large industrial city in south-western Poland, the Nazis were looking for the rabbi - they had this crazy idea that Jews were led politically by rabbis. Anyone who knows Jewish tradition knows that the rabbis had a spiritual task. Very rarely did a rabbi lead a community, certainly not in Poland. People consulted with the rabbi, but that is something different. So in Czestochowa they contacted the son of the rabbi and he said 'My father, no, he does not know how to lead a community. He knows how to decide religious questions'. So a man who had been one of the leaders of the Jewish community before became the head of the Judenrat, and he appointed the others - a coalition of people. In Lodz it was completely different. In Lodz there was an elderly man, younger than I am now but older than most of the community, who was a widower, who had been a leader of the General Zionist party in Lodz, and who had been fired from that party in 1937 as a member of the Jewish community council because he had made an alliance with the antisemitic Polish government. He was a renegade Zionist, if you like, and he was sitting in a committee meeting when German soldiers marched in and asked who was in charge. And he said 'I am', and he became the head of the Lodz Judenrat. He became a dictator. There was no council there. Rumkowski was a brutal dictator.

The man in Lublin, Mark Alten, was a kind, devoted man who tried to do for his community whatever he could. The man in Czestochowa, Leib Kapinski, was a man who permitted the organisation of Jewish trade unions in the ghetto to demand more bread, and tried to satisfy their demands. And in the area of south-western Poland there was another concentration of Jews, mainly in two sister towns, Sosnowiec and Bedzin, and the man in Sosnowiec was a Zionist who thought that this was an opportunity for his group to take charge of the Jewish community. His name was Moshe Merin and Merin was another dictator opposed by social groups and resistance groups within the ghetto. You see, completely different stories. You have probably heard about the way that Elchanan Elkes became head of the Judenrat. He did not want to become the head of the .Judenrat; there was the persuasion of a venerated rabbi in the community - Rabbi Schmukler - who decided that he was the right person and everyone agreed. And after much pressure Dr Elkes agreed to lead the Judenrat and is considered by practically every Kaunas/Kovno survivor to have been a saintly man. But a person who was not elected, who appointed himself in the Vilna ghetto, which is just a few dozen miles from Kovno, which is the capital of Lithuania now - it used to be in Poland - the man who emerged as being in charge was another dictator, Jacob Gens, but a dictator who got the support of the community, different from Rumkowski in Lodz, different from Merin in Sosnowiec. Can you say that all these people were the same? Can you say that all you are interested in is the murder, and not the intentions and the actual actions? There is an example that fits Hilberg's thesis; in Lithuania there is the town which in Lithuanian is called Shiauliai and in Yiddish is called

Shavli. Shavli is a medium-sized town with a not very large Jewish population before the war, and they built a hospital, - well, there was a hospital there; when the ghetto was established, of course the hospital was not included, and so they had to establish a hospital. And what Hilberg could say was "What did the hospital do?" It preserved the lives of Jews so long as the Germans wanted it, in order to do what? Basically to preserve them for slave work for the Nazis directly, or if it was a family member so that the family member who slave worked for the Nazis would slave work better if he/she knew that the relative was being cared for. The moment the Nazis decided they were no longer needed everyone was killed - the people in the hospital, the doctors and nurses first. So the hospital was part of the Nazi bureaucratic machinery that killed Jews.' The example is very good. The answer to it, of course, is not only that the Jews when they founded the hospital did not know that, but mainly that the purpose of the hospital was to save lives. The fact that these lives were lost later on is something that we know now; it was the task of a humanistic society, of a society that cared for its members contrary to the Nazis, standing in absolute opposition to the Nazi morale - or morals if you like. To preserve life as long as possible, and that is what they did.

Now let me give you an example of my own. The example is this. The head of the Lodz ghetto was Chaim Rumkowski. At first of course he and the Nazis did not know what the ultimate plan would be, but very early on he decided that the only way he could guide the group through the war - there were more than 160,000 Jews there - was to make them work for the Nazis because it stood to reason that slave owners do not kill their slaves; it is counter productive, and it is not cost efficient. And so he established in the Lodz Ghetto a large number of workshops that worked for the Nazis. Now he was right in that because the main reason why the Nazis did not abolish the Lodz Ghetto was because the Lodz Ghetto produced uniforms and boots etc. for Nazi soldiers, for the German army. In 1942 at some point, probably pretty early on, Rumkowski became aware of the so-called 'final solution', in other words of the German plan to murder all Jews. We know this because we have a testimony of an anti-Nazi German who penetrated into the Lodz Ghetto and interviewed both Rumkowski and a rabbi who supported Rumkowski from a moral point of view, and Rumkowski's chief of police asked this anti-Nazi German 'I know that they want to kill us, and my policy is (a) to work for them so they will kill as few of us as possible, and (b) when they demand people I know where they are being sent to, but I prefer to be responsible for sending a certain number so that others may be able to survive. What shall I do? Shall I continue with this?' and the anti-Nazi German said 'I can not answer such a question. You should never be in a position to ask me such a question, and I do not know what the answer should be, but I in your place would act the way you are doing.' And in September 1942 Rumkowski was responsible, personally responsible, for sending for murder – and he knew it – up to 10,000 children under the age of 10, and there is a speech that survived, because it was taken down by a stenographer, in which he says clearly that he knows that the children were doomed to die – the community knew it, he told them – and then he sent his underworld criminals, Jewish criminals, his strong men, to tear the children from their parents. But in the late spring of 1944 the Lodz Ghetto was the only ghetto in Poland that had survived. No other ghetto had survived by then, and it survived because they were producing things that the Germans needed. And so there was opposition on behalf of the German civilian authorities in Lodz to the destruction of the ghetto. Now the Soviet army in the meantime began occupying Poland from the east, liberating Poland, and in July 1944 when there were still 69,000 Jews in the Lodz Ghetto, the Soviet army came up to the Vistula river on the eastern suburb of Warsaw, Praga, which was occupied by the Soviet army. The Soviets stopped at the Vistula river for reasons that had nothing to do with Jews, Holocaust, Lodz, or anything else. For their own reasons. Seven months later, in January 1945, the Soviets re-started their offensive and in three days occupied Lodz which is exactly 100 kilometres, 60 miles, away from the Vistula river, as the crow flies. But by that time the 69,000 Jews of Lodz had been killed. In August, one month after the Russians had stopped at the Vistula river the Germans had destroyed the ghetto of Lodz, shipped it to Auschwitz and left in Lodz a group of some 760 Jews who were given the task of cleaning up, clearing up, the Jewish property that was left behind in the Lodz ghetto. All these Jews were liberated by the Soviets because the Germans had other worries in those three days than to deal with those hundreds of Jews. They were all liberated. I am now asking the question; 'Had the Soviet army not stopped at the Vistula river – for its own reasons – but decided to go forward another 100 kilometres in July 1944 and liberated Lodz with maybe tens of thousands of Jews still alive, would we then have established a memorial for the great Mordechai Chaim Rumkowski for being the only Judenrat head who managed by his policies to rescue tens of thousands of Jews? Or would we have made a public example of him and hanged him from the highest gallows for having sent 10,000 children to their death?' That is the dilemma; that is the real dilemma.

Now as I speak, or maybe in another hour or two, when you think about it, you will make your judgement. You will say 'I can not judge', but you will judge because you have no choice. And that is the real issue of the Judenrat, of that kind of Judenrat. Not the kind of non-dilemma that my friend Hilberg proposes. Now you will ask me what my judgement is. My judgement is that I have the greatest difficulty; that I agonised over it, but I had no choice - the same as you have no choice - and I would have hanged Mordechai Chaim Rumkowski for having sent 10,000 children to their deaths. He had no right to do that. But it is a dilemma. You see each such Judenrat, in places not only in eastern Europe - there was a Judenrat in Amsterdam, there was a Judenrat in Belgium, there were two Judenrats in France, there was a Judenrat in Slovakia, there was a Judenrat in Budapest which was in fact the Judenrat that represented Hungarian Jews - they all behaved differently from one another, and in order to point to the extremes let me go from Lodz, which is an extreme case, to others. Amsterdam is just like Lodz, because in these places not only did the Judenrat yield to the Germans but acted in what Hilberg rightly calls 'anticipatory compliance'. In other words, they complied with Nazi orders before the Nazis even gave them. And the other extreme? There was a Judenrat in Minsk. How did that Judenrat come into existence? After all there had been no Jewish community under Soviet rule since 1917 because the Soviets of course destroyed all Jewish communities, but there were Jews in Minsk, large numbers of them. The story may or may not be true, that they took a group of Jewish men for slave labour and then an officer came and said 'Who can speak German here?' Nobody said anything. Then there was a threatening stance by this German officer and one man came forward and said 'I can speak German'. His name was Ilya Mishkin and he was a water engineer of the Minsk municipality before the war. He became the head of the Judenrat. 'You are the head of the Judenrat, nominate your Judenrat.' And he did; he had no choice. From day 1 the Judenrat led by Mishkin was a resistance group; not only the Judenrat, even the Jewish police, which in most ghettos in eastern Europe was a very bad group of people, belonged to the resistance. In Minsk they collaborated with the Judenrat and the underground resistance was headed by a man by the name of Hersch Smolar. These were not Zionists, not member of the Jewish Socialist Party in Poland, certainly not religious. These were Jewish communists, and Smolar was a Jewish communist from Warsaw who was a refugee in Minsk, and Mishkin got in touch with Smolar. Mishkin became the arm of Smolar in organising Jewish resistance. How did they organise Jewish resistance? They realised they could not possibly resist in the ghetto that the Germans set up in Minsk, but Minsk is next to forests – a huge jungle, where if you do not have a compass you can die simply because you do not know your way because you can not see the stars, and when you climb a hill there are trees on the hill, too. There's no way that you can see where you are. There are swamps where you would go in and never come out again. In Russian it is called a 'pushcha'. In these jungles there were Soviet partisans, not really friendly to Jews; they were usually scattered Soviet soldiers who had been surrounded by Germans and escaped into the forest and led some kind of a life there. And then they became organised to resist the Germans, and Mishkin got in touch with these partisans and, to cut a long story short, within eighteen months they managed to smuggle out some 7,500 Jews into the forest to fight the Germans. It is the largest Jewish resistance activity under the Nazis, quantitatively speaking; much larger than the Warsaw ghetto rebellion. Most of these people did not survive. They were either killed in the forest' sometimes by the partisans, sometimes delivered to the Germans by the local population, sometimes killed by the Germans in big actions that the Nazis did in these forests, and sometimes because they simply did not know how to exist in the forest, 7,500 people. Those who survived fought the Nazis with arms in hand. As to the ghetto itself, the partisans sent their wounded to be treated in the Jewish hospital in the ghetto; they came in with a Jewish star, and then they were treated. And to conclude this story of the Minsk ghetto, because parallel things happened in other places, the Germans caught a Belorussian on the non-Jewish side of Minsk; they tortured him and he said 'the man who leads the Jewish resistance in the ghetto is a man by the name of – not Smolar because Smolar had an assumed name – Stolarevich' which in Polish and Belo-Russian means a carpenter. Smolar was now being sought by the Germans. The Germans came into the ghetto and said to Moshe Yaffe, Mishkin's successor, 'unless you deliver to us Stolarevich we are going to kill every Jew in the ghetto', and what happened was that Yaffe found a man who had been murdered that day. They completely destroyed this man's face and the man was covered with blood, and then they took Smolar's false identity card under the name of Stolarevich and they put it in the blooded trousers of this man and then they called the SS in and they said 'Look, we've found Stolarevich. He's dead'. The Germans searched the pockets and they found the identity card under the name Stolarevich and Smolar survived. He died about two or three years ago in Israel, no longer a communist and completely forgotten.

Now that was a Judenrat too, you see. There were Judenräte in towns in eastern Poland that organised rebellions against the Germans. For instance in a place called Tuczy where there were 2,500 Jews led by a man called Gecel Schwartzman who organised the resistance of the ghetto. They burned the ghetto the moment they saw the Germans coming in and then they attacked the Germans with axes and with the one rifle they had. I could go on and on. There were different kinds of Judenräte.

How do you explain the differences? I think that the differences lie in a number of factors. I think the crucial factor is the difference of individuals one from another. I think people simply react differently from one another to extreme situations. There are people who can resist when you never would have believed they could, and people who do not – you never would have believed they would not. There was the community tradition that played some part, not everywhere, not in Minsk – there had been no community there. And there were communities where there was a community spirit and the leadership did not follow it at all. But it worked in some places; also the Nazi pressure was different in different countries of Europe. It was easier to resist the Nazis in Belgium than it was to resist them in Hungary. It was relatively easier to do something in Slovakia than it would have been in Poland. So that is another factor. And then the timing is terribly important.

Was it at the beginning of the war, was it at the end of the war? We found – or rather Aaron Weiss, who I mentioned before, found, when he examined 107 Judenräte in Poland – he found that of the first group of Jewish councils, i.e. the ones who were first appointed by the Germans, 70% and over got a clean bill of health by all the survivors from these communities, and usually what these survivors said is 'the Judenräte were generally very bad, traitors, but our Judenrat was OK', because the general image of Jewish survivors of the Holocaust was that all Judenräte were traitors. Then when you examine the particular Judenrat from which they came you find that there is a contradiction. Over 70% said 'Our Judenrat was fine. Why? Because it tried to help, because it tried to rescue, because it did not deliver Jews to the Germans', and so on. There was a second .Judenrat in many places because usually after a certain period of time the Nazis dismissed the first group. 'Dismissing' usually meant murdering them. And then they appointed a second group. The second Judenrat in most communities got a very bad report by the survivors. About 30% said that 'Our Judenrat was OK, even under the second leadership' - exactly the other way from the first one. In many places there was a third and even a fourth Judenrat. Almost everywhere these Judenräte were collaborators with the Germans, under tremendous pressure and hoping to survive themselves.

I want to end with a story, because a historian is a person who tells stories – stories that are documented. A historian who does not tell a story is, in my eyes, not a historian. He is a chronicler who chronicles what happened. I want to tell you a true story which shows you the dilemma of Judenrat and resistance. The name of the place is Kosow Huculski – there are plenty of places in Poland called Kosow, and one of them is in the area near to the Tatra mountains. It was a Jewish town of some 2,5000 or so Jews - quite well off actually. The Jews there spoke the civilised language of German because they had been under Austrian rule prior to World War I. There were some industries locally; they were sort of lower/middle-class people. And there was a Judenrat there like everywhere else and by 1942 they knew perfectly well what the Nazis were up to, and on Passover/Pesach - because the Nazis always did their murder actions on Jewish holidays - they got a phone call. One of the peculiar things is that the Nazis did not cut the telephone wires, not even in the Warsaw ghetto, it was very peculiar, nobody can understand why. They got a phone call from a Polish friend of Jews and the phone call told them 'There are several trucks with SS people, armed to the teeth, already in Kosow Huculski. It will take them a few minutes to get to the Judenrat building. Obviously they are intent on a murder action.' Because it was the eve of Passover there was a meeting of the Judenrat just then, and the head of the Judenrat of Kosow, Chaim Steiner, said 'Everyone run to your home and try to hide' (because people of course had prepared cellars and hiding places and so on) 'or find a Ukrainian peasant with whom you can stay. Try to do anything you can to save your family.

Run. Only those who have real guts stay with me.' Three members of the Judenrat, plus the chairman, stayed on to meet the Germans. Why did they want to meet the Germans? Because they knew by then when the Germans came they did not have a plan of the place, they wanted to know (this was not a closed ghetto) – where the Jews live, they wanted to have statistics, they then want to put the guards around the place so that the Jews could not escape. All this takes time – usually one or two hours. So four members of the Judenrat were going to meet the Germans in order to give time to the others to try to escape or to hide. One of the members of the Judenrat, as they waited for the Germans, fainted and collapsed and when they resuscitated him the head of the Judenrat said 'Go home. There's no point in you staying here.' And three men of the Judenrat of Kosow stayed behind to meet the Germans. And I ask, 'Is Hilberg still right? Is that not as though they had resisted with arms and even more so?' And you may ask 'how do we know the story?' It's very simple. The Germans did not come. They went to another place. Kosow Huculski was murdered at Rosh Hashanah in September 1942 and not at Pesach in April. And in the meantime, people wrote down the story.

It is events and stories like that which make you realise the real dilemma of leadership groups who had no options to speak of because if they chose the resistance option they knew they would die, and if they stayed on they knew they would die. It was a different kind of death that they could choose, but by summer 1942 they knew perfectly well, except if they lived under illusions, that that was the choice, or lack of choice they had. Were there other groups of Jewish leaders who were not members of the Judenrat who organised outside of the Judenrat on the one hand and the resistance groups on the other? There were, but that would be a subject for another lecture.

Surviving the Holocaust: The Memory of the Holocaust in a Post-Holocaust World

Deborah Lipstadt

It is a pleasure being here. It is a pleasure being in the United Kingdom and being anywhere but a courtroom. This is the actually the first time I have spoken in front of a large British audience on the trial, and it's nice to be able to assume that you know certain things that American audiences don't know. Very often I will be asked at lectures in the United States, 'Well how could this man bring a law suit against you? What about the First Amendment?' And I always point out that the First Amendment is the First Amendment to the American Constitution, and you have neither a First Amendment nor a Constitution - much to my dismay. And the other factor of course is to tell you — and this may be an example of bringing 'coals to Newcastle' - that your libel laws are the mirror image of my libel laws. I do mention that, however, because it will give you some sense, and many of the questions from fellow historians have been 'How has this trial impacted on me?' and to bring you back to the beginning.

In Fall 1995 I first received a letter from Penguin UK, my co-publishers, my co-defendants — they were the first defendant, I was the second defendant — informing me that David Irving was considering suing me for what I had written about him in my book, *Denying the Holocaust: The growing assault on truth and memory*. In the book — those of you who have seen the book may know that the book is essentially an analysis, a modus operandi, of deniers, their history, who they are and how they operate. It is not an attempt to answer deniers point by point. I didn't think that was necessary; I didn't think that was needed. But I was more intrigued by how they make their arguments and how people react, particularly students and particularly college campuses. The focus of the book was not only, but primarily on the United States. In the book, which is approximately 300 pages in length, I make brief reference to David Irving and I essentially say about him that he is (a) a holocaust denier; (b) that he is someone who knows the truth but bends it so that it should fit his ideological objectives; (c) that he is a Hitler partisan, someone who is anxious to exonerate Hitler, to wipe any of the blemishes off Hitler's record. I make these statements and I call him also 'the most dangerous of holocaust deniers'. The reason I describe him so, again something well known to you, is that he had a reputation as a writer of historical works separate and apart from his reputation as a denier. There is no other denier who has that status or reputation, not even the one who is a professor at North-Western University in Chicago. He is an electrical engineer, so you would question how his training as an electrical engineer would equip him for historical research.

But David Irving was someone who came to this topic with the record of having written quite a few books, mainly about aspects of World War II, etc, books that are primarily known to you. What's interesting about Irving's work is that even before becoming a denier he 'comes out of the closet' as a denier in the late 1980s. In 1988, at the trial of Ernst Sundel in Toronto, a holocaust denier against whom the Crown, the Canadian Government, had brought a case, he openly presented himself to the court as a holocaust denier. But before that, even in his earlier works, you could see certain consistent themes which I will greatly summarise because this is not an analysis of his work and if you want to see these themes developed more extensively you're welcome to visit a web site on the trial which has all the transcripts, the judgements, the expert reports — www.h.org — and on that you'll find in one of the expert reports (Richard Evans) an analysis of Irving's writings on history. If you look at them there are certain consistent themes that flow through them, and I apologise to you for greatly summarising them, but basically one could see that in all these works the Allies presented as worse than you would think they were, the Third Reich presented as better than you would think it was, that whatever happened to the Jews was most likely not the work of the upper echelon of Third Reich leadership, and that on some levels the Jews may have deserved whatever it was that happened to them. And the books are written — and Irving acknowledges this - by and large from the perspective of the Third Reich. For instance, in *Hitler's War* he says 'I wrote it as if I was sitting at Hitler's desk and seeing how the war was waged'. Now there's nothing wrong in itself with that, but it's the other things in the book that raise questions about its historical validity. But at the Sundel trial in the late 1980s he actually comes out and says 'I question now whether there was a holocaust; I question whether there were really gas chambers, etc. etc.' He very much promotes the report by Fred Leuchter, an American 'gas chamber expert', but he's hardly that — we have this barbaric thing of killing people — sometimes even the wrong people — the death penalty in the United States, and Leuchter developed a system for lethal injection. But if you've seen the documentary by Errol Morris, 'Mr Death', on Leuchter, he's a very strange man. He goes to Auschwitz and claims to come back with a report that shows that the gas chambers were a scientific impossibility. But, of course, as soon as you look closely at the report even a lay person trained in chemical, or engineering, or science background can pick up many questionable features. Leuchter in this report which Irving not only adopts but publishes here in the United Kingdom with a glowing introduction, says things like 'you compare the amount of Zyklon-B used to supposedly kill humans in gas chambers and the amount of Zyklon-B that was used to disinfect people's clothing and objects — it was used for both purposes — and you see that much more was used on the clothing to kill the vermin than was used to kill the humans, so obviously it couldn't be a valid system. The claims about Zyklon-B had to be false.' Well, anyone who knows even the least bit from your own experience — I used to live in California, and before you could sell a house in California you had to have it tented and then they would spray the contemporary equivalent of Zyklon-B to kill the termites and other vermin that might be in it, and I talked to the company that was doing it (I happened to be there when they were tenting the house) and I asked them 'how long could a human being last in the house?' and they answered 'for a very short time'. So I asked 'why do you have to have it tented and have the gas going in for such a long time?' and they answered 'because it takes much longer to kill the vermin. That's a given scientific fact.' So, plain and simple, Leuchter got it wrong in that he went into the gas chambers and carved out, even though they are Polish national monuments, a Polish historical site, just took a chunk out of the wall of the plaster and the brick behind it, put it in a bag and sent it to a laboratory in the United States that does chemical analysis for industry. He didn't tell the company what was present or what it was from; he just asked them to check for the presence of hydrogen cyanide. And the company did what it does when it gets objects and has to check for the presence of a chemical — it pulverises the matter, adds certain chemicals, and monitors the chemical reaction to see if HCN is present or not. Well they did that and reported that there was no residue of Zyklon-B present, so Leuchter trumpeted that by saying 'See, in the places where there were supposed to be gas chambers there's not remainder of this gas'. Well you would know if you've been to the gas chambers at Auschwitz, with the exception of Gas Chamber 1, the ones in Birkenau are rubble so they had been exposed to the elements for 40 years by the time Leuchter did his work. So they would already have led to a certain lessening of the presence. Subsequently, the man at the laboratory was told what he was testing for — that these were supposedly the walls of gas chambers and they were being tested for the presence of HCN. Then he said 'our test is totally worthless because HCN would barely penetrate into the plaster. What we would have had to do in order to do a proper test would be to shave off a very thin layer of the plaster and test that. But the minute we took the plaster and brick behind it and pulverised it we diluted the presence of any HCN by a factor of thousands.' So the test is a worthless test. But these are the kind of things that Irving proposed and presented to the world as raising serious doubt that there were gas chambers. Look at his editions of *Hitler's War* — *Hitler's War* is the book which though he written quite a few books before that, brings him most dramatically to the world's attention. He argues in the 1977 edition that Hitler didn't know about the holocaust and that it was done against his will by underlings and that it was done without his knowledge. When the book is re-issued in 1991, in another edition, the holocaust has been eliminated from it and when he is asked why the holocaust isn't there — in an interview he even volunteers the information — he says 'if something didn't happen you don't even dignify it with a footnote'. He talks about the gas chambers as 'Disneyland for tourists', as 'a legend'. At the Sundel trial when he testified he said to the judge 'I have no reason to believe that there were gas chambers or a holocaust'.

Given all that, when I received this letter in the Fall of 1995 informing me that he was considering suing me for libel, I laughed. Inappropriate reaction. I laughed first of all because at that time I didn't know about the vagaries or the idiosyncrasies to me of your libel laws which in contrast to the ones in my country — we may do some things wrong but I think we get libel better than you do, though reasonable people can differ on that — in the United States had he threatened me with libel he would have had to prove that I indeed had libelled him. Here the burden was on me to prove that I did not libel him, and that immediately changed the complexion of the case. There were many people who said to me 'Ignore it'; my lawyer friends laughed or were appalled. They said 'It's very easy for them to say when they haven't been threatened with a libel suit'. Then other people said to me 'Write some sort of apology to him which is not really an apology which will make it go away.' Of course had I just ignored it there's little chance that he could have done anything to me personally, given that my assets, such as they are, are in the United States, but that was not the motivating factor. The motivating factor was if I had not fought it Penguin probably would not have fought it either, though I'm not sure about that, but there's a good chance, and then he would have won and he could have said 'a High Court in London accepted my version of the holocaust as a legitimate version'. His version of the holocaust of course is that Hitler was not involved, there was no plan to kill the Jews, certainly six million Jews did not die. Maybe some did die, but most of them — as he has said many times — including. I was reading this morning when writing my book on the trial, in Australia he says 'Many hundreds of thousands may have died at Auschwitz but most of them died of typhus and disease and things like that'. His numbers always wandered all over the place. So that there was no plan; there was no systematic killing; any Jews who were killed on the eastern front were killed as a result of rogue actions by criminal elements of Germans, Latvians, Estonians, Lithuanians, Ukrainians, etc. And of course the survivors are all either consciously lying about what happened to them or they are sick people, and they have a psychiatric problem and they just pick up this story and spread the story. My assumption is that there may well be some survivors in the audience and it's painful to hear these things. It's even more painful to hear him pronounce these things in the court room and know that there were survivors in the public gallery listening to this. Some of you may have read in the paper on the first or second day a woman was present. She went up to him at the end of the day and she said to him 'Mr Irving. My parents died in Auschwitz.' And his response was 'Madam, you will be pleased to know they didn't die in gas chambers.' Why she should be pleased about that I don't know, but that was his response.

So number one, the burden was on me to prove the truth of what I said. Number two, in the United States in libel law if you can show that you took information from a legitimate source — another book, not a book that has not been immediately panned as being a bogus argument or being based on fraudulent material, or from a reputable newspaper — then you are considered 'safe'. But here, even if I quoted from some place else and all my comments on him were based on other sources, both primary and secondary, it wasn't enough. I had to be able to prove that the people writing knew that what they were writing was the truth. So that was another difference. The final difference —just a small diversion into the comparative legal systems, and then I leave that because that's not what you came to hear about — is that in the United States he couldn't even have fought this case (a) because of the First Amendment, which is freedom of expression, freedom of the press, etc., and (b) because the Supreme Court which sometimes decides things right (it got Florida voting all wrong!), decided in a case in the 1950s called *Sullivan v The New York Times*, that a public figure — this makes it very different from your system — now by that they were talking primarily about politicians, but they included in that interpretation authors who write and put themselves in the public eye, cannot sue for libel unless they can prove malicious intent; that the person writing knew that what they were writing was wrong and maliciously went ahead and did it anyway to cause damage. That is why we don't have politicians being able to sue newspapers all the time, as you sometimes have here in the United Kingdom. So I was obviously quickly brought up to speed on the differences in the law and realised that this was something that had to be addressed quite seriously.

Now I don't believe that David Irving ever thought the case would really come to trial. I think he thought he would just write this letter, Penguin would withdraw the book, he would get an apology from me or from Penguin, and he would get a flurry of publicity. And much to his surprise first Penguin's lawyers, and then I took my own solicitors — Anthony Julius and James from the firm of Mischcon de Reya — because I thought it was wiser to have my own. In any case even though Penguin was resolute, not in my defence, but in defending the book which they had published, they are part of a one of the largest publishing companies in the world, one of the major corporations, and one never knows what kind of decision will be made, how those decisions will play out, and it just felt smarter to have my own solicitor. I didn't take it because of anything they did, but to be sure of pro-active steps in my defence. In any case, we decided early on, Anthony Julius, James and myself, and then Penguin lawyers agreed with this, that this would not be and could not become a case about 'did the holocaust happen?' If it became a 'did the holocaust happen?' trial then any victory we would have achieved would have been a Pyrrhic victory because we did not feel that any judge or jury — we weren't sure at the beginning whether it would be just a judge or a judge and jury, as it turned out it was just a judge — was needed to prove that the holocaust happened. Nor did we feel that would be the issue at the heart of this trial. The issue at the heart was 'Was what Deborah Lipstadt wrote about David Irving correct?', There are two ways of responding to libel; either you are misinterpreting what I wrote; you're putting a false slant in a defence; let me argue what it really means, or you can argue, yes, You're interpreting exactly right, and it is true', and that was the nature of our defence. That what I had written about David Irving was the absolute truth and therefore it was our responsibility and our forensic strategy to go about proving that it was true. And how would we prove it was true? We would prove it was true by putting his work under the spotlight, turning his historical work essentially into the defendant, and show that absolutely this was a man who consciously lied about World War II, consciously lied about the holocaust, consciously misrepresented things, consciously falsified, etc. etc. And we went about proving that, and as you may probably know from the judge, Judge Charles Gray's judgement, we proved it in a quite stupendous and forceful fashion. He called Irving essentially a liar, a holocaust denier, described his interpretation of history as fanciful, and totally dismissed Irving's claims that these were just mistakes. One of the points we wanted to show, and as any historian will admit — some have admitted publicly others not — any good academic will admit that we all make mistakes. None of us has written books that when another person pores over them doesn't find some mistake. But if they are genuinely mistakes, over the course of a lifetime some will go in one direction, some will go in another direction, depending what your particular argument is or what your particular area will be. What we wanted to demonstrate to the court — and did demonstrate over and over again - was that with Irving's so-called mistakes when we backed him into a corner and he couldn't argue any more that his interpretation of a particular document was the correct interpretation, then he would say, 'Well I made a mistake'. But what was interesting as we argued in our final submission is that all his mistakes moved in the same direction — exoneration of Hitler, exoneration of the Axis, blaming the British, blaming Churchill, blaming the Jews, diminishing what happened to the Jews, etc. It was always in that direction. So our strategy was not to let it be a 'Did the holocaust happen?' trial, but a trial of Irving as a historian. And once we reached that decision other strategic or tactical aspects of the forensic part of the case fell into place, and that would be that we would not call survivors to testify. Now there are some people who would have liked this to call survivors to testify; there were many survivors who came forward wanting to testify; but we made a decision on two grounds not to do that. First and foremost, on a forensic ground in that bringing survivors as witnesses to testify was as if we had to bring people to prove that this thing happened. We didn't feel we had to prove that this happened; we felt that was a given. Second, since David Irving was a litigate in person, representing himself, we didn't feel it was ethical to ask someone who had faced the holocaust in any way, particularly if they had been in a death camp, to have to go into a stand and be questioned by Irving. It was just a conversation, but to be questioned by him where he would control the questioning and obviously his objective would be to demonstrate, or to try to demonstrate, to present this person to the court as someone who didn't know what he or she was talking about, that if they said a Hungarian arrived in Auschwitz in the spring of 1944 on this particular day, and he would say 'Well do you know on this particular day something else happened there, or how could this be?' Maybe it did happen, but the person might not have known about it, etc. and we didn't think that was an ethical thing to do. So instead, because we weren't out to prove the holocaust happened, we assembled what can only be described as a dream team of historians, led by Richard Evans of Cambridge, Peter Longerich of University of London, Christopher Browning of the University of North Carolina, and Hajo Funke of Technical University in Berlin — all of them historians with the exception of Professor Funke who, is a specialist on right wing extremist groups in Germany to show Irving's connections with neo-Nazi groups, etc. To go back to prove that my statement that he knows the truth and he bends the truth for his own ideological purposes, Irving once described himself as a mild fascist; I would say that's like being a little bit pregnant — either you are or you aren't! But he wanted to prove that he had these political objectives. And then we engaged in the discovery process and that really was the key. One can read the brilliant and wonderful reports by the experts and the excellent presentation of the case, the outstanding presentation of the case, in court by Richard Rampton serving as both my barrister and Penguin's barrister, the excellent work done by Heather Rodgers, Penguin's junior barrister, by my solicitors, but the key was in how we went about discovery.

Essentially when Irving presented his first discovery list -which I think had about 2,500 items on it -what became pretty clear was that this was a boilerplate discovery list. Now many of us keep on our computers boilerplates. I travel a lot so I have boilerplate instructions for house-sitters, people who will take care of my house when I'm gone. If it's the summer I have to change it for the air-conditioning; if it's the winter I have to change the instructions for the heating; but the other instructions are pretty much the same — who to reach in case of emergency - if one set of friends is out of town I'll switch phone numbers; but it's a boilerplate. I know of no-one with a boilerplate discovery list of items to introduce into litigation, but this clearly was a list that had been prepared for some other case as much of it had nothing to do with what I had written or what was being argued. We went through the case with a list and we immediately discerned what was absent, what was missing, what was there as unnecessary for us to have go through and still there for whatever reason, and then things that were only there — a letter to, but not a letter from — and then what was absent — correspondence we expected he would have with leading neo-Nazis and others, and just ask for that. And suddenly we were barraged with an avalanche of information, of documents, by him from his files which he was forced to turn over. We also asked for his diaries. It was a known fact that he kept a daily diary; he was adamant against giving us those diaries even though he described himself in court — I think it was on the fourth day —as 'being one of the most generous of plaintiffs of claimants because he even turned over his diaries to us'. It took us two days in court to get them in pre-trial hearings before a sort of junior judge, and essentially the argument that Anthony made in court was that I claimed that he kept company with neo-Nazis, with right wing extremists, and we had a right to see whether that indeed was the case, and the diaries would reveal that.

Now one of the important things of this case was all the information that was revealed both from the documents and from the diaries, and I have to say that my own personal perspective early on — and again our forensic strategy — was to prevent this from going to trial. Any good lawyer, even when they have a fabulous, strong, wonderful, air-tight case prefers not to go to court because there are always unexpected, unanticipated kinds of thing that will happen. But we went about fighting aggressively initially in order to prevent that from happening by assembling this amount of documentation, by having these experts do these reports, all the while preparing interrogatories which the only way Irving could answer them — because they were based on documentation — was either by 'yes, I lied' or 'I didn't lie', and I will give you some examples about that in a moment. All the while expecting that at some point he would say 'I'm dropping the case', and he would use the excuse 'I can't withstand the power of being brought by Penguin with Pearson behind it (the mother company) and Deborah Lipstadt' — my great power, of course. He argued that I was part of the international Jewish conspiracy. Any of those of you in this audience who are the least bit familiar with the Jewish community know that Jews can't agree on anything, much less have a conspiracy. And he could never quite decide — by the way, and I don't say this at all humorously, though sometimes people find it humorous, I don't mean it humorously at all — in addition to being an anti-semite of the first order and a racist of the first order, this man is also a misogynist of the first order, and he could never quite decide whether I was the head of the conspiracy, because he couldn't quite see a conspiracy this powerful which could stop him from publishing and doing his work and accusing him of being a denier being run by a woman. So sometimes he described me as being head of the conspiracy and sometimes he described me as just an operative — following orders as any good woman should. But in any case we were hoping that he would at some time just give up and we wouldn't go to trial but my attitude — and I think the legal team as well — began to change as we came closer to the trial and as it became clear what material we were discovering from his personal files —materials he had to turn over, the materials we were finding in his diaries because what we also got from the court was a vast collection of video and audio tapes of him making speeches, not just interviews he had given on the television and on the radio that would have been accessible probably through the archives of these particular stations, but speeches he gave privately, films, speeches of him speaking at rallies in Germany, one rally in Harlow where when he finished speaking there was a sort of who's who of holocaust deniers and anti-semites speaking about this rally, and when he had finished the audience began to chant 'sieg heil, sieg heil'. It was pretty chilling to see that. And of course the information we found in his diaries of his association with people of my country such as David Duke, a former leader of the Ku Klux Klan whose book he edited, with whom he exchanges fund-raising lists, with whom he plays tennis when he comes to the United States, along with the leader of the National

Alliance — one of the most racist, anti-semitic groups in the United States, with racist, anti-semitic groups here — Ian Hancock and others here in Britain and in Germany and in Australia and other places. I began to feel rather than hoping he would drop out, suddenly I found myself shifting each day. Instead of hoping for a phone call from the lawyers saying 'he's dropped the case', to fearing that phone call because none of this information could be part of the public record had he dropped the case. Anything we would have discovered from his diaries, from the video tapes — well now they all are public. Let me give you one or two examples of what we meant by showing these were mistakes. Richard Evans describes Irving's work as a 'tissue of lies'. Professor Evans talks about how it's full of mistranslations, of inventions, or words said by somebody attributed to somebody else, dates reversed, etc. etc. And it is interesting early on before Professor Evans actually began to do the research at one point — we hired him as an expert witness — his testimony and expert reports were really written for the court — and there is only so much you can tell him what you want him to research, and we told him we wanted to research Irving as a historian and early on made a offhand comment to him that he should really argue that Irving isn't a historian at all — because while historians take many different approaches in doing their work, he violates the most basic norms of our honesty in reporting what he finds, reporting voices which conflict with his opinion, being true to the sources, etc. And Professor Evans said to himself and Anthony Julius 'That's not an efficacious approach to take; that someone who has written 20-25 books at that point is not a historian.' So when you read historical experts saying something is not efficacious you drop it because of course they have to be writing independently. And that's why when I read his report and discovered in the opening pages he writes 'in no way can David Irving be considered a historian'. He corroborates his opinion through the documentation, through following the sources, through tracking the footnotes — with the help of two wonderful graduate students without whom we really probably could not have done the work that we did. They really were absolutely vigilant about tracking down documents. But there would be things like in Irving's book on Goebbels, where Irving said that Goebbels was not an anti-semite until he came to Berlin in the latter years of the Weimar Republic, encountered Jews there, encountered them involved in all sorts of criminal activities and that this turned him into an anti-semite and consequently after that whenever Goebbels talked about Jews he would talk about Jews as criminals. Then he goes on — now the voice of Irving the historian weighs in as he goes on to write in the book, and he says 'Unfortunately Goebbels was not entirely wrong', and Irving goes on to give statistics that say in 1933 so many pickpockets were reported in Germany and of those pickpockets so many were Jews; and there were so many cases of this crime, and so many were Jews — he gives a number of statistics — and the final statistic he gives is that in 1933 alone while there were 31,000 cases of fraud, mainly insurance fraud by Jews. Then he gives a footnote and four sources in the footnote; two are books in German on crime in Germany during the period in question — we read the books, we went through the books — there's no reference there to any of this information. And the first two sources in the footnote of the four sources, one is Interpol as cited by the DNB — the DNB was the Nazi party press office, a propaganda office. Interpol was created right after World War I as an international criminal tracking bureau, its headquarters were in Vienna and as a result of the Anschluss the Third Reich took it over, it was moved to Berlin under Heinrich's control, and it became anything but an international criminal reporting bureau. It became an arm of the propaganda agencies of the Third Reich. So when you say Interpol you're not talking about pre-World War II Interpol or pre-1930 Interpol or post-World War II Interpol; you're talking about an entity which really is an arm of the Nazi party of the Third Reich. And the DNB is a Nazi party press bureau, so to cite them as a source for the statistics —without at the very least telling your readers says the following: caveat , reader beware. A good historian would cite if you're using a questionable source or writing about the Soviet Union and using a source on dissidents, then I would use the KGB as a source but I should identify who the KGB was/is and let my readers know. The second source in the footnote is a man named Kurt Daluger, and it says 'Kurt Daluger, cited in' and it gives a date of 1935 and then an archival/documentary reference. And when we tracked this down Kurt Daluger was very interesting feature in the court; we knew of course before going into court as it was in Evans' report, Richard Rampton said to Irving who was in the witness box 'Mr Irving, tell me who Kurt Daluger was'. And he said 'Kurt Daluger was the head of the Ordnungs police; a sort of reserve police, and he was already the head in 1935, he was a committed Nazi', and Richard Rampton, who is of Scottish origin, said 'Oh Mr Irving, tell me a wee bit more about Kurt Daluger'. 'Oh Kurt Daluger goes on to be a killer on the Eastern Front, part of the

Einsatz Commando units, and he's hung after the war, punished by the Czechs (I believe it is) for his activities. So it's a bit of a dodgy source' but Irving uses him as a source on Jewish criminal statistics. Essentially what was Daluger doing in 1935 that Irving used him as a source? Daluger convened a press conference in 1935 for foreign journalists, and essentially said to them 'You're always criticising us about what we write about Jews, but you never ask why we write these negative things about Jews. Well Jews are criminals. Let me give you statistics', and he gives these statistics just like Irving reports them in the book, and his final statistic is '... and in 1933 alone there were 31,000 cases of fraud, mainly by Jews'. Daluger said '31,000 cases of fraud, mainly by Jews'; when that statistic appears in Irving's book it is '31,000 cases of fraud, mainly insurance fraud, by Jews'. Insurance fraud has parachuted into first place in the sources, and Daluger who has qualified this 31,000 cases, saying 'mainly by Jews', but not all by Jews, that 'mainly by Jews' now modifies the insurance frauds and all the cases are by Jews. So, essentially Irving has out-Nazied the Nazi in his statistics about Jewish crime – total fabrication of what is.

Let me give you one or two other examples before I begin to draw this to a close. At one point Irving in a number of speeches and press conferences and in his book on Nuremberg, he cites the testimony of a French woman, a French Catholic woman, who was a prisoner in Birkenau – she had been a member of the resistance – who gives testimony at the Nuremberg trials – Marie Vaillant-Couturier. And this woman gives testimony at the trials because of certain things she had seen from the window of the women's barracks in which she was at Birkenau. And at one point in her testimony before the Nuremberg tribunal she says there was a barracks in Birkenau which was used as a brothel by the SS officers. Then she goes on to say in the next sentence, 'such was the case in all the other camps, barracks used as brothels by SS officers'. At which point one of the American judges at Nuremberg, Judge Francis Biddle, who was the Attorney-General of the United States who had been sent by Truman to be a judge at Nuremberg, in his transcript of her remarks, said 'This I don't believe. She had only been in Birkenau so anything she said about other camps was essentially hearsay.' When Irving talked about her testimony in his press conference speech, and in his book on Nuremberg he has a picture of her with a big stamp on it, 'Credibility Denied by the Judge'. He talks about her, he says 'The judge writes in the transcript "All this I don't believe".' Then at another point in his speech Irving says 'Judge Biddle was so put off by what she wrote that he wrote in his diary transcript of the testimony "She's a bloody liar; I don't believe a word she is saying".' So first of all we went back to Biddle's archives to see what was indeed said, and we also went to Irving's house which we had on discovery, and we questioned Irving about this and we said 'Mr Irving, the judge wrote "This I don't believe", not "All this I don't believe".' And he said 'Well I copied it down wrong'. We said 'No you didn't; here are your notes. You copied it exactly right.' Then he said 'Well you know, when I gave that speech saying he wrote "'She's a bloody liar", I had been in the Biddle archives months, even years, before - four, five, ten years before - how can I remember what Biddle had actually said?' We said, 'Mr Irving, according to your diaries you had been there only shortly before.' At which point he turned to the judge and said 'This I don't believe; all this I don't believe. It really doesn't make a difference; it's author's licence.' He was saying that to a judge about what another judge had written, and the judge said 'No, Mr Irving, I think it does make a great deal of difference.' We did this over and over again. Now some people may say it was overkill. We felt that it was incumbent upon us to fight this case as if it was the most serious commercial case that could come before lawyers; that we couldn't fight it on a wing and a prayer, just by chance hoping the judgement would be - that this man was a liar and clearly falsified history, and I can give you numerous other examples of his doing that. We felt that it was necessary not because of any intrinsic importance of David Irving. David Irving is not very important. Fighting David Irving, Anthony Julius likes to say, is like getting rid of the dirt you step in on the street, left over by some four-legged beast. It has no intrinsic importance unless you drag it into the house; then it can cause you great problems and great difficulties. The point is to get rid of it before you go into the house, to clean it off. So the achievement we had was not so much the victory but the not losing, although in the victory itself the strength of Judge Gray's comments, even with the judicial restraint that he showed, were really quite overwhelming. This was a case I think when history performed very well in the court room. I don't know that history would always perform well in the court room. It performed well in the court room partly because we were so well prepared, partly because this man had left such a paper trail and such an obvious trail of lies and misrepresentations, of changes of date -he had a record of a meeting between Hitler and

Horthy the head of Hungary, in April 1943 – berating Horthy for not having come down hard on the Jews and acting more severely towards the Jews, and Irving writes 'Well of course Hitler was concerned about the Jews being in Budapest because this was the time of the Warsaw Ghetto uprising'. Well, this meeting took place four days before the Warsaw ghetto uprising. Now someone who would know that the Warsaw ghetto uprising was in the middle of 1943 might not have known the exact dates. But what of course Irving is trying to do is show that Hitler may have said strong things about the Jews, but he had a right to be concerned; it was a legitimate right because the Jews had had this uprising in Warsaw. Also in that meeting – that meeting was over two days – and the first day Hitler sort of plays 'good cop' and Horthy says 'Well what do you really want me to do? Deport them to camps?' Hitler says 'No, that's not necessary'. And the next day Hitler says 'You can deport them to the camp like beasts'. Irving reverses the two meetings so that the meeting concludes with Hitler taking a very conciliatory stance on what the Jews did. And Irving says 'Of course, I just made a mistake and wrote what happened on the first day, happened on the second day?' But again and again he showed these mistakes as they were.

The Past in Future:
History, Memory and Representation

Stephen D. Smith MBE PhD

The Holocaust is still contemporary history, though not for much longer. Time is going by; for some it is running out. The Holocaust recedes into the past, but also proceeds with the present. Its presence in our cultural discourse, in its varied forms, will continue to be a dynamic entity in our midst. The question of this lecture is, quite simply, what kind of entity is it in our sense of history, in our memory, and in our representations of it? And what can we expect in future?

1 The Past Present

The past is what you make it. That is, the past we know and speak of is a past reconstructed, with the benefit of hindsight and the convenience of analysis. The past is one of those things we live with that shape us, that tell us who we were and by extension, who we are.

The past once was: but is no more. It was fact, but in the present is more than fact alone. It was entire, but is always partial. It dwells most completely in the mind, but is only indelible in form. It is present, but never the present. It is true to itself, however true we are to it. At once we respect it and disregard it; teach it and ignore it; hide it and flaunt it. We contort it, stretch it, bend it, deride it, and run away from it, even though it is always receding from us. The past is never behind us, but always and only before us. We shape it, and it shapes us.

The past is present and absent, tangible and abstract, true and false. It is not constructed but re-constructed. Not told, but rather re-told, re-written, re-presented – in our language, with our forms, for our times. Whatever it was, it certainly isn't.

The past is many things. For the purposes of this account, I want to observe two fundamental components of the past as happening and reporting. Happening is the occurrence of the event itself. Reporting is what is said about it. What happened, and what is reported about it, are two different events. Both occur in the present – but the present is different for each. The actors, the audience, the purpose are entirely different during and after.

The event that happened and the report of the event are both conditioned by their context. The happening is conditioned by say, geopolitics, economics, culture, action, in action, and of course the aims and intent of those making it happen. The report is conditioned by contexts too; such as authorship, occasion, audience, genre, politics, language, assumptions, presumptions, politics, sources, access, knowledge, and again, the aim and intent of those who are reporting it. Therefore, while the happening remains the same, the report of it will vary.

It is the past that is reported, not the past that happened, which is the past we know. Unless of course, what happened, happened to us; but even then our report of what we experienced will always be an insufficient, incomplete rendition of that which we experienced.

Which begs the question, 'who really is in command of our past?' There is only one way to influence the happening of history – and that chance occurs when it is in the making. Influencing the past through its reporting, however, is open to anyone who wishes to imagine or reconstruct that past and to author their own version of its truth.

To imagine the past is not unlike dreaming in reverse, I guess. A retrospective reconstruction in curtailed, fragmentary elements, that may or may not be connected, laden with our own noise and at times, nonsense. It is a set of highlights, key moments – the goals and near misses, if you like – all patched together to make narrative sense, with our own commentary overlaid. The past we imagine and report is always potted history, milestones, vistas, sketches, which can tell you virtually nothing about the real-time experience of life and death, laughter and sorrow. It merely confirms that there once was life and death, laughter and sorrow, and with it some of the conditions that precipitated their happening, descriptions of the events, qualitative reflection on the relative value of the events and analysis about their consequences.

But whatever we say, we will always be selective, as the past is conditioned by what I choose to disclose. I select events and shape words to describe them in the way in which I understand them. A third party examining the same timeframe or scenario may well select different events or describe the same events in different words. But, what is it that drives the privileging of one event over another? What makes it stand out more than the event that occurred before it, after it or alongside it? What is it in the present that suggests that a particular happening in the past is worthy of reporting to you? Is it about documentation; the process of justice; the purpose of entertainment; the justification of political ideology; the facilitation of education; the pursuit of fact, or its falsification? How do I select that which may be important for you to know? Do I select by what I think you may wish to hear – or not hear? How do I trust the selection I make – and can you? Does this not point to the fact that reported past is therefore an entirely fragmentary imaginary re-creation of what I think you ought to know about what happened?

As an Honorary Fellow of the Stanley Burton Centre for Holocaust Studies in the History Department I have to watch my step here before I am flung off the campus for historiographical heresy. However, this is an important place to start when we approach the dangerous history of the Holocaust, because the value of millions of lives depends upon the way in which we represent their story in our retelling of its history. If it was my life, I would want to know that writers and readers were sufficiently aware of the insufficiency of their discipline to treat it and therefore me with respect. Being frank about the nature of reported past is precisely to underpin the endeavour of securing the past in future, because if we do not know the weaknesses of our representations, how are we to be sure about their strengths? If we do not know the line beyond which there is falsehood, how will we know what is true? If we do know the difference between ideology and sociology, history and mystery, then how will we know that what we are saying aids the cause of knowledge and dignity for those whose lives our history represents?

2 The Holocaust as Past Present

The Holocaust occurred in the past. It happened, and then came the reports of what happened after that.

What happened is arguably beyond words, let alone within the scope of full and accurate reporting. What form of words can you use to adequately describe a mass grave brimming with people who only hours before had wanted to live? What kinds of expression does any language contain to craft a sentence endowed with any sense of meaning describing a gas chamber full of people, all of them either sons or daughters, mothers and fathers, brothers and sisters of another human being, all extinguished while gasping for air in a darkened concrete room, with hundreds of others clambering for that last gasp of oxygen? Rudolph Reder, one of only two inmates of Belzec to survive the war, grapples with this very point.

I heard the doors being shut; I heard shrieks and cries; I heard desperate calls for help in Polish and in Yiddish. I heard the blood-curdling wails of women and the squeals of children, which after a short time became one long, horrifying scream . . . Words are inadequate to describe our state of mind and what we felt when we heard the terrible moans of those people and the cries of the children being murdered.[1]

Primo Levi and Charlotte Delbo support the impossibility of describing such brutality. 'We became aware that our language lacks words to express this offence, the demolition of man',[2] says Levi and, Delbo in fewer words still, 'Everything there is inexplicable.'[3]

And yet, the work that has now been published about various aspects of the Holocaust rivals any other period of contemporary history in sheer volume of text. There is a question, however, about the relative sufficiency of these documents to cover the scope of the events and to provide enough analysis to give them any reasonable chance of carrying adequate meaning. You might be surprised just how often I go to the library to find information on a particular topic about the Holocaust only to find a remarkable deficit of basic knowledge around the issue concerned, let alone any secondary analysis.

Right now, I am making a documentary with the BBC and Kitty Hart-Moxon about the last six months of her incarceration under the Nazis. This is the six months following her evacuation from Auschwitz to the point of her liberation a thousand miles away, six camps later. Her experience included the shunting back and forth of inmates in the confused final months of the war, sometimes on foot, at other times in trains – the death marches. This set of events involved hundreds of thousands of inmates, and the deaths of an estimated two hundred and fifty thousand[4] on the kerbs and sidings of Germany's collapsing empire. One would have thought that such significant historical events involving the deaths of so many civilians would be well documented, with maps and diagrams and routes and statistics. Unfortunately we have had to re-discover this history ourselves, to dig out of the landscape the clues that help to piece that journey together. There are no books to guide us, no signposts, and scant clues to suggest where or how this seemingly unimportant event took place. This is not a criticism; it is just an indication of how little we still know.

Then there is the extermination camp of Belzec, whose total victim number had never properly been established. The working figure was always 600,000. This is what you were told in the Encyclopaedia of the Holocaust.[5] This figure was not inaccurate, it was just accurate about something that had not been verified. Then, three years ago, a team of archaeologists resorted to drilling cores to determine how wide, how deep and how long the mass graves had been, in order to calculate how many bodies they had contained.[6] Following the study the number of victims of the Holocaust went up by 200,000, and that in the closing year of the century that massacred them and over 170m others.[7] And those extra 200,000 souls got a line in the broadsheets.

Then there are the names. The most basic identity tag that every person has is a name. What happens when you do not have a name? Simply, you do not exist. Names are also the basic tool of the historian. Historians document the interaction between people. Therefore, without names, arguably there is no history. How do you describe the life, the actions or death of an individual with no identity? No name; no victim; no life; nothing lost, is the gruesome equation.

By 1998, Yad Vashem had collected 'pages of testimony' containing the names of two million people who were victims of the Holocaust. Among the 55,000,000 pages of unpublished documents at Yad Vashem, there are also 12,000 lists containing approximately 18 million names; names which often re-occur several times on different kinds of lists within the collection, which it has not yet been possible to cross-reference. This is the largest verifiable collection of data on victims of the Holocaust anywhere.[8]

147

By a sweet twist of irony, it was Swiss banks that helped to start the process of making these names truly accessible, when in 1999 the Volcker Commission invested in a six-month exercise in computerising and cross-referencing records at Yad Vashem with those held by the banks in Switzerland, in order to establish which accounts had belonged to victims of the Holocaust. In order to know who the dormant accounts belonged to, there had to be names against which they could search. Without a list of names there were no account holders, but there was evidence in their possession to suggest that those people must once have existed, as their accounts were in their names. The only way they could constructively match names to victims was to have a verified victims list, to see if they were there. Yad Vashem and an army of students and volunteers trawled list after list of names from community records, local archives, private collections and survivors' memories, name by name, from over 12,000 sources. As a result, records of approximately three million victims can now be accessed on computer[9]

So the events themselves are still veiled and highly complex, but our cultural normalisation of them has already boiled them down to almost nothing. 'The Holocaust' is a singular proper noun. It describes an entity, an object that has been named. But that is not what these events were. 'The Holocaust', that short word that means little to most people, was actually a series of millions of events that meant a great deal to everybody affected by them. Condensed into that term are frightened children, anxious mothers and bewildered fathers. There is survival and betrayal, hope and hopelessness, courage and fear. On the part of the perpetrators, there is evil and cunning; day after day there are thousands of conscious acts of deception, confusion and brutality. And millions of bystanders chose to watch and then watch again the next day. There is a bullet and a gun, a spade and a hole. There is a train with coal, money to make it run, men to make it happen, people to clean it down when the journey was over and its cargo gone. Every day, for five and a half years, there were desks, memos and orders and shiny boots and knocks on doors and howling in the street. There was a murder, then another murder, then another, and the corpses piled high one at a time. These are the facts, and there are millions of them.

So what is this thing we call The Holocaust? Is it the killing of a five-year-old in the Ukraine or an eighty-five year old at Belzec? Is it about quantity, quality or intent, about individuals, systems or outcomes? Is the anti-Jewish boycott of 1933 part of it, or the Nuremberg laws of 1935, or the Wannsee conference of 1942? What do we include in this simple-to-say mirage of a term, which divorces most of us from its reality? It seems to have the unnerving effect of reducing our discourse around this most demanding of subjects to, "Oh, yes, the Holocaust, terrible, terrible, and it still goes on today, doesn't it?!"

By creating a term, have we insulated society, or even inadvertently obfuscated the events themselves? Have we buried the life of the victims in the mass grave of history too? Whatever that series of events was, they were clearly not identical to what they have become. Now we have our museums, our documentaries, Holocaust Memorial Day, theatre, music, the big screen and shelf after shelf of text on endless views on fashionable topics; the Pope, the Gold, and Goldhagen of course.

The question is, when this round of books are read and left to collect a generation's worth of dust, and the last survivor dies, what kind of history, what kind of memory, what kind of representations will conduit this past in future?

3 The Future of Holocaust History

The writing of history, however deficient, however subject to authorship or manipulated by the moment, is a vital element of the future of the past. The writing of history is a discipline. It takes skill and perseverance to eke out seemingly trivial detail in pursuit of reclaiming past actions. In face of the daunting task of piecing together the never-ending scattered fragments of the Third Reich, taking time to understand a single mechanism, a particular order, a specific series of inter-related events, takes singular determination. There are more enticing, less demanding subjects that an historian, who is after all a free agent, can do other than to stare endlessly into the detail of someone else's misery. So we owe these professionals a debt of gratitude, no matter how we despair at their persistent reliance on hard facts and documents, sometimes with little creativity; or at the other extreme worry about their creativity with assumptions that cannot be proven based on the evidence they have. Either way, it is these texts that will shape the knowledge we develop over time.

The writing of history is a dynamic, organic process in which the historiographical development of any given set of events undergoes continual change. No less so, the Holocaust. New opinion and points of view; new evidence that sheds new light; a new theory borne out of newly understood compound relationships between events previously known, but not previously deduced.

This past will continue to undergo change influenced by other emerging forces too. The archives retrieved from the Soviets have hardly begun to be tapped. There is likely to be endless material that has no significant impact upon what we have already known for a long time, or merely confirms that which was deduced a generation ago. There will be new finds, most insignificant, others more demanding, that may even force a rethink on certain aspects of the policy or implementation of mass death in the Third Reich.

So too, new generations read their ancestors' pasts in different ways. The current generation of prominent German historians, such as Peter Longerich, Michael Geyer, Christian Gerlach, Ulrisch Herbert and Gotz Aly, to name but a few,[10] are treating us to a new form of post-war-generation German historiography. They are not so bound-up in its direct consequences, but being native to the country that spawned the detail they seek to uncover adds added force. It has its drawbacks, too, because their identity is also bound up with whatever conclusions they draw. Either they can divorce themselves from the country their parents once contributed to, or they impose a break in the continuity of national identity, which is difficult for any national history to entertain, never mind sustain. And so they are creating a heavy burden to bear, which not everyone in Germany will want on their shoulders. They may tell it, but whether their society wants to hear it is a different matter altogether.

And so we see that history is much more than information organised neatly to demonstrate facticity; it is a social, cultural and political enterprise in which the identity of writers and readers is also bound up. That is, what we read, what we see, what we know and understand is in part conditioned by who we are and what is happening to us now, and in turn it conditions us, or confirms something about the condition we are in.

Right now, I have the privilege of working with the Education Department at Yad Vashem on creating a book on the role of perpetrators during the Third Reich. This text charts the experiences of a range of people and examines a number of case studies. It particularly observes the process that lead to their participation in the events of the Holocaust and the dilemmas and choices they faced, as well as the actions they took. It is a demanding book because it asks questions about human nature, the moral boundaries of people, the propensity to follow peer groups, to be pushed by leaders and pulled by ambition, or by the capacity to dehumanise a fellow human being, consciously or otherwise. The text self-consciously asks readers to question motives, examine roles, and think about consequences. It is a text designed to make people think about how easy it is to become a perpetrator, or at least to fail to recognise the events in which one is bound up and therefore a participant. The English version of this text will appear shortly, printed in Israel and jointly published by Yad Vashem and Beth Shalom. Interestingly, a Hebrew translation of the book is not being made available to Israelis. Read into that what you will, but it raises interesting questions about Israel the State, Israelis the people and Yad Vashem the institution and their complex inter-relationship. This is not a criticism necessarily, nor a general statement about Israeli policy, but rather a reflection on what any of us are prepared to say, to whom, when and why.

Whatever subtext, the text itself will continue to benefit from other new resources. In the former Soviet Union, former occupied states such as Lithuania, Latvia and Estonia have created Historical Commissions in order to examine more closely what actually happened in their own countries. This is important because there is an abundance of previously untapped local source material, which brings new insights to light daily.

I particularly want to highlight the work that has been going on in Lithuania, because this was a country besieged by accusations about its inability to face the past. It was rightly disgraced for rehabilitating war criminals and failing to confront its current antisemitism, and condemned for its outright, persistent denial of the scale of Lithuanian involvement in the killings. Whether or not Lithuania now has a firm grip on all of those issues demands further examination, but over the last few years it has gone through a transforming revaluation of its history and has moved a considerable distance towards establishing one of the most significant national memorial projects anywhere.

In the process it had to confront its history in a new way. In September 1998, President Valdas Adamkus signed a decree forming the 'International Commission for the Evaluation of the Crimes of the Nazi and Soviet Occupation Regimes in Lithuania.'[11] The logic was to place the two evils together, neatly balancing what would be seen by the population as Fascist, a.k.a Nazi, and Communist, a.k.a. Jewish, crimes in their country. Israelis refused to sit on the international panel on the grounds that while both occupations are important to understand, they are not the same thing, nor can they be traded. In bringing its committee together, Lithuania had to separate parts of its history that had been two sides of a popular narrative coin – and thus restate its own identity. It created two committees, one dealing with the Nazi period, the other with the Soviet periods. It sounds easy, but the revision of this historical socio-political positioning was history in its own right.

Alongside this challenge and the rich source material that has come with it, there is an added benefit. Local historians in Lithuania, now reviewing their sources, are starting to re-write the history they first wrote diligently for the Soviets just half a generation ago, then re-wrote for Lithuanian national re-identification ten years ago. Some of the honesty emerging is refreshing. Professor Ludas Truska from Vilnius University confesses that he set out to demonstrate that indeed, as popular opinion had long stated, the Jews had played a disproportionate role in running the administration of the one-year Soviet occupation of Lithuania prior to the invasion of the Nazis in June 1941. By deduction, they would also have been disproportionately responsible for the deportation of ordinary Lithuanian citizens to the Siberian Gulag in the spring of 1941. The implication is transparent. If the Jews were responsible for the Soviet occupation and the deportations of nationalist-leaning Lithuanians, then they could not complain when the Nazis, assisted by Lithuanian revolutionary nationalists, carried out horrendous so-called 'reprisals' against the Jews in late June 1941.

Truska went to the archive and discovered evidence that did not square with the narrative of many of his compatriots, who were sure of this version of their national history. Bravely, he admitted his own shortcomings at pre-empting his findings, and demonstrated through his new representation of that historical period, that in fact Jews had been disproportionately represented as there were marginally less Jews in the administration in Soviet Lithuania than there were in the population per capita.

Today, less than ten years later, Lithuania has an entirely different history of that period in its own language, accessible through its own libraries and bookshops. Shortly one would hope that the writings of Truska, Eidintas, Brandišauskas[12] and others from Lithuania will be translated into English, so that those of us that have been shielded from – God forbid – Lithuanian historians, will benefit from their research and their unique historical collections and perspectives.

So whatever our history of the Holocaust is now, it will continue to proliferate. Some will tediously re-examine; others will find new insights that help us to revise and reorient our thinking. Either way it is set to continue, unlike the collection of memoir-related sources to which we now turn.

4 The Future of Holocaust Memory

Survivors have become the visible evidence of the perpetration of genocide on a whole group of people. They are the embodiment of the reality we seek to touch, but cannot. They symbolise the humanity, the suffering, the determination. They bring us close to the dead and at the same time give us hope for the future. They are a link to the past and a lifeline for our despair. We ignored them for more than two generations and then when we re-discovered them as frail old people, who had endured a lifetime trapped with their memories, we suddenly we wanted to hear what they had to say. Now, in every school and university campus, survivors tell their story and give a whole generation an insight into the period that destroyed their lives forever. I am reminded that Sara Elkes, who stoically makes this lecture happen and lends the name of her murdered father to its title, does not attend the lecture, to avoid the flinching reality of that which we discuss together this evening. This is her life, and although time goes by, the memory of the offence does not alter fundamentally. The wound is just as deep as it always was.

For these people, there is an imminent end point of their narrative and personal memory. At that point there will be much more to say, but whatever was not said will be silenced finally and for always. Therefore, quite simply, there is no future for the memory of individuals, except in the texts, the audio-visual testimonies, the drawings, the sculptures, the letters and the talks that have either been published or penetrated the memories of another generation. But there is a discourse that will follow this final silencing. The question is whether we have gathered enough material to feed that discourse for perpetuity.

The Survivors of the Shoah Visual History Foundation has collected over 50,000 audio-visual testimonies of survivors. With an average of 2 hours per tape it would take 48 working years to watch the collection, or 11.4 years viewing at 24 hours per day. This mass of documentary evidence will keep historians, educators and curators in supply of testimony for many years to come. Through this the Holocaust has become without doubt the event most contributed to by its eyewitnesses victims ever.

There are concerns about memoir sources. They revolve around accuracy, around interview techniques and a variety of worries about the validity of testimony as an historical source. These concerns tend to target testimony and testifiers as the point of weakness. However, the weakness is not on the part of testimony, which after all is only an extension of the memory of the individual. The weakness is on the part of some historians and readers of the Holocaust who fail to understand the nature of testimonial narrative. Testimony is a document, but it is not squeaky clean like a piece of paper. It moves and shifts with time. It can be wholly inaccurate and absolutely true at the same time, because memory is not based around the same parameters as a card file index.

That said, survivors who give their testimony should be prepared to have their testimony scrutinised like any other document.[13] But those of us who examine it have to understand that just because one part of the testimony has slippage, it does not necessarily discredit either the testimony or the individual, unless every one of us in this room is prepared to be branded an unreliable, lying twister of the past. This is how memory and its consequent narrative works. To deconstruct the testimony of a survivor, to compare and contrast the development of ideas, the change of detail or the obvious misreading of the history in which they were involved, is a simple intellectual task. What is much more demanding is how one incorporates those convolutions, inaccuracies, and fault lines into a competent reading of testimony, to take those experiences as we find them and make then a part of our future, with care and compassion.

If we are interested in the long-term impact of survivor testimony on our thinking and our response to the events they attempt to describe, the question is, have we asked enough questions – that is, have we asked the right ones?

The chronological life histories in which survivors tell their stories, what happened before, during and after, is important to document. But is that all that survivors are? Are they not people, with lives and emotions, opinions and points of view? While we stand on the outside and try to make sense of their experience with all the powers of our analysis, is it not the case that they have been closer to this for longer than any of us and have had to struggle to make sense of it in their daily lives? How did they square becoming a mother when having no mother, eating bread in a world where previously it was the absolute source of life, seeing love and laughter in a world of hate and fear? Do we know what these people think? Do we know what they have to tell us about ethics and emotions, about families and communities, about the propensity of human beings to hate and to kill? Do we know yet what they felt like as victims; what they feel like today?

If testimony is an extension of the life of the testifier; and if testimony is a choice; and if testimony is limited or facilitated by the context in which it is given, is there not reason to suspect that we should stop treating survivors as a phenomenon of another age? Are they symbols alone, or should we provide them with the opportunity to give voice to their experience, to be themselves in our presence, to share in their lives, not just their words?

This future is particularly imminent. And the future of testimony brings its load of silence, where all that was unspoken will be condemned to a world of unborn words, formed but never voiced. That is when the Final Solution will finally be final. When, as survivor Batsheva Dagan describes it, 'the Last Train leaves the Station',[14] there will be no more conversation and what we have will be what we have. And there will be no more.

Testimony remains open, but not open to abuse; to transmutation; to intellectualisation, transforming its message to a different age for different people with different views. It says what it says. It is consistent, even when it varies; it speaks as one person speaks to another, and to have it is to respond to the trust invested in it.

Words are only a part of testimony. The rest will cease to exist; body, mind and spirit will go, and all we will have are the narrative bones. "Videos can't answer questions. I can," Batsheva said to me one day.[15] Nor do memoirs, documentaries, empty chairs in school halls or benches in memorial gardens dedicated to the deceased.

And so there is a simple imperative to emerge from this. If there is a question to ask, ask it, while there is opportunity to hear an answer, because that answer might well form a part of their past in our future. Eventually and inevitably, when the last survivors die, whatever they wrote will remain as their memorial to the dead. Then the responsibility to maintain the mandate of the dead will be, and is being, deferred to those who did not experience its offence. This will be an altogether more unpredictable memory, with an even more demanding mandate to fulfil as speech turns to silence once and for all, and we are left to hand on the message through our various representations.

5 The Future of Holocaust Representation

Most of us are neither survivors nor historians, but may want to say something about the events of the Holocaust and their consequences. We may wish to find ways of expressing this through art or drama or literature, giving form to the feelings we have, the stories we have discovered and the message we want to convey. These in their multiple variants we call representations.

All of us access the events of the Holocaust and their consequences through a spectrum of representations. Some of them are created under academic discipline, others out of personal grief, and yet others are blatantly commercial products delivered through commercial channels to reach a popular audience. Some are laden with passion, some distorted by political rhetoric, others still are the concoction of fertile minds deftly able to weave into narrative or film the beauty of art and the power of mass death. Some are clearly successful at delivering their message, some fail to impress. Some are obviously amateur; some so highly polished, they don't feel right. All of them have a text and a subtext – that is, a form and a motive.

These 'things' that we have created to convey these events and their consequences are all around us. However much we think they are important, we need a critical eye to appreciate them. That said, we also need to accept them for what they are and what they can tell us. Representations of the Holocaust include historigraphical narratives, and therefore like them are conditioned by the context in which they are formed. They must be read against their backdrop and understood as a product of the people, the politics and trends of the times in which they are formed.

The discussion around the Holocaust monument in Berlin was not about the willingness or otherwise of the Germans to admit their past – no one has been accusing them of that – but of the message they wanted their memorial to deliver to future generations. Something as solid, as large and as permanent as that, is going to shape or at least condition the social and cultural climate in which it sits, or if it does not it has failed. Discussion actually revolved around whether it should be monumental or educational or both.[16] Clearly the discussants were aware that a memorial is only as good as the knowledge base of the public that views it – unless it contributes to that knowledge base in the process of their interaction with it. This does not make it a museum, but a memorial place, where people learn. In the creation of the Beth Shalom Holocaust Centre this was a trick that we learned fairly early on, as we too created a memorial centre in which people come to learn.

Our creation of representations, with all their inherent weaknesses, is in and of itself part of the learning process. On a regular basis I watch school students form a response to their visit to the Beth Shalom Centre through poetry, creative writing and works of art. In so doing pupils transform their newly acquired knowledge into communicable form. There is good reason to state that scant knowledge is in no position to create any form of representation about the events of the Holocaust, because of its in-built limitations. But this is how society learns, takes on identity and relates to circumstances in such a way that it owns a part, if

157

only a part, of the representational landscape as a personal response. In the process I also believe that transformation takes place in the individual, that is, the process of finding words and committing them to paper transforms knowledge into identity in a permanent or at least semi-permanent life-affecting manner. So our representations teach us, however limited the form as a means of containing the message.

There are to be more representations. There are as yet unborn artists, fifth generation children of survivors, countries still that are yet to come to terms with their past, that in future will wish to express parts of this history to their own generations in new ways. But there is a danger that comes with this avid proliferation. Too much of something may not necessarily be a good thing, even if, as in this case, one can not do enough to convey the story.

The Holocaust is not a history to grow used to and yet with every book, with each new monument or museum, with a national memorial day and an international task force for Holocaust education, we are growing ever more used to the presence of the Holocaust in our cultural landscape. As we do so, its significance will fade and consequently its challenge will diminish. It will become increasingly mythologised, relativised, contracted, and précised to fit our soundbite society which ordinarily allows approximately half a sentence to relate the full force of the Holocaust and its demands upon contemporary society. The day we grow used to the Holocaust is the day that the lives that were wasted then will be doomed to oblivion forever.

There are more representations to follow. We would be more concerned if there were no representations; but they are only as useful as our reading of them, which leaves the value of their future in our hands.

6 In conclusion

My conclusion is that I have no conclusion, or at least that there should be no conclusion. Conclusion brings closure; an end to our struggle. Closure will mean that historians will have said all there is to say and made their final analysis. And yet we know there is so much we need to discover and many questions we have not yet even asked about what happened, how and why.

Closure will mean that survivors are silenced, or at least a line drawn under their memories and their meaning reduced to a series of convenient bullet points. Memories that should never be bounded by arbitrary lines will be circumscribed and contained by our limited appreciation of the many layers of unseen meaning.

Closure means that we are confident we understand what happened and what it means and what we should do with what we have learned, because we have learned it well.

But surely there can be no conclusion to our struggle, to our questions, to our grappling with traumatic past such as this is.

But though I advocate we go on with this infinite task, I do so with caution, because we must always check our work against some principles.

Theory is easy, but this is not an intellectual exercise, even though we should use our intellect to capacity. To turn the events of the Holocaust into an academic exercise may be dangerous unless we do so with caution and compassion. At the heart of the work we do must be an integrity based on a genuine desire to fathom the tragedy this represents for all of us. The victims should be lent dignity, the survivors supported, the young enlightened through this work. Any activity which is an end in itself will be a dead end, of no value, perhaps even of negative value.

That said, we must always be rigorous. The lives that were wasted were sacred, as is every human life. But the text of the Holocaust is not a sacred text. Therefore we must read it carefully; question it, compare it, struggle with its implications, write it and then re-write it if we must. We must also be rigorous with ourselves and not allow our context to dictate the content, but assist the content in challenging our contexts.

And so I conclude that we should never conclude our struggle to learn, our struggle to question, our commitment to ask, and then to begin all over again. There is no doubt that if my generation is curious to know what happened a generation before, my children's generation will want to know too. There are those who deny its existence, but their calumny will always be marginal if we faithfully tell it as it was. The Holocaust has happened, and that will not change.

And so there is only inconclusion, which makes me think that there is a place for the past in future – to make our future uncomfortable, to make us nervous about who we are and what we do. There is only inconclusion, because there was never justice, and until there is justice, the dead will never rest, so why should we? There is only inconclusion, because there is unfinished business for all of us while ever there is suffering in the world; there is only inconclusion, because this account is never closed, circumscribed or completed.

The dead will always be dead. There is no get-out clause, nor any justification to suggest 'that it was not in vain'. It was in vain; those lives were wasted, and there is only despair for those who died in despair and those who were sentenced to live with it the rest of their lives. This is not something to forget and move on from. There is no salvation, no happy end, no sunset to walk into, no certainty of a better future. And so our history, our memory and our representations must never allow us to escape into the comfort of conclusion. They must always be there, to make us think; to challenge our future with our past.

1   Extracts from 'Belzec', by Rudolph Reder, translated by M M Rubel and published in *Polin: Studies in Polish Jewry* (vol. 13: Focusing on the Holocaust and its Aftermath). ed. Anthony Polonsky, The Littman Library of Jewish Civilization, London 2000.

2   Primo Levi, quoted by Irving Howe in *Writing and the Holocaust,* pp.175-199 edited by Berel Lang (London: Holmes & Meier, 1988).

3   Charlotte Delbo, p.266 *Auschwitz and After* (London:Yale University Press, 1995).

4   Shmuel Krakowski, 'Death Marches', p354 *Encyclopedia of the Holocaust*, ed. Israel Gutman. London: MacMillan, 1990

5   Yitzhak Arad, 'Belzec', p178. The figure 600,000 is also cited by, among others, Nachman Blumental in 'Belzec', p454, *Encyclopaedia Judaica*, ed. Geoffrey Wigoder and Cecil Roth. Jerusalem: Kater Publishing House; and Martin Gilbert, p169, *The Dent Atlas of the Holocaust*, London: J. M. Dent, 2nd Ed. 1993. While research carried out in 1999 showed that the actual figure was substantially higher, the figure 600,000 was again quoted in 2001, in the 'Belzec' entry of *The Holocaust Encyclopedia*, ed. Walter Laqueur, New Haven:Yale University Press.

6   See 'A Reassessment: Resettlement transports to Belzec, March-December 1942,' Robin O' Neil, 1999 (http://www.jewishgen.org/Yizkor/belzec/belzec.html).

7   Professor Rudy Rummel has calculated that between 1900 and 1987, over 169m people died as a result of state-sponsored mass murder. See http://www.hawaii.edu/powerkills/20TH.HTM.

8   These details regarding unpublished lists of names at Yad Vashem were provided to the author by Yaakov Lozovick, Yad Vashem.

9   For information about the Volcker Commission's activities, see http://www.geneva-finance.ch/e/volcker.htm.

10 Peter Longerich, Royal Holloway College, London; Michael Geyer, University of Chicago; Christian Gerlach, Technical University, Berlin; Ulrisch Herbert, University of Freiburg. Gotz Aly may not currently be holding a university post.

11 See http://www.komisija.lt/

12 Recent work includes, L. Truska, 'And forgive us the trespasses of our parents and grandparents. On the Holocaust in Lithuania in 1941', *Kultūros barai*, 1999, Nr 5 pp62-65; Nr 6, pp 55-58. A. Eidintas, ed, *The Case of the Massacre of the Lithuanian Jews: selected documents and articles.* Lithuania: Vaga, 2001. V Brandišauskas, 'The Holocaust in Lithuania: historiographic situation and principal problems', *Metraštis,* volume 14, pp135-152, Lithuanian Catholic Science Academy, Vilnius, 1999; 'Lithuanian Activist Front, Provisional Government and the Jewish Question', *Lietuvių-žydų santykiai. Istoriniai, teiseiniaia ir politiniaia aspektai* (Lithuanian-Jewish Relations. Historical, legal and political asects), Vilnius, 1999 pp17-21

13 From personal conversation with Professor Aubrey Newman, March 2002

14 From personal conversation with Batsheva Dagan

15 Batsheva Dagan, video testimony, 11.02.99

16 http://news.bbc.co.uk/hi/english/world/europe/newsid_377000/377841.stm

Epilogue

Barbara Butler

There is a story told of a dog who lived in his family for many years and when he died the family members were so heartbroken that they decided to have him made into a rug, which they would always have with them. Everyday they would be reminded of their beloved old dog. The idea worked fairly well so long as the family members who remembered the dog were alive. Every time they walked through the room where the rug was placed they were reminded of the dog, and when they sat down in the room in the evenings they were able to think about him. But the day came when the people who remembered the dog died, and then the rug meant very little to those who lived in the house. After many years the rug became thin and ragged and the new people who bought the house decided to get rid of it. The house was cleaned and the rug was thrown out of the window, where for one brief moment, it moved in the breeze, and the old dog fleetingly reappeared.

There is the danger that we who read and learn about the Holocaust today are like the people who never knew the old dog. We may know about what happened in our heads, but be largely unaffected in our hearts and therefore in our lives. We may actually read the history of what happened, taking in the many dreadful facts, without the knowledge affecting our lives or our world. We may know of the tens of thousands of Jewish people who were murdered in Lithuania for example, of the way they were forced into the ghetto in Kovno where they were subject to forced labour for three years before being sent to concentration camps where most of them died. We may know all this and we may not make any connections to ourselves, we may not change or become active for reconciliation and peace.

Most people in the early 21st Century World, may sadly fail to learn the lessons of history and of human nature, so that the horrors of the past will reappear, albeit in a new guise. There have been many horrors following the holocaust, including the suffering of the people in Vietnam in the 1960s and 70s, and the murderous rule of Pol Pot in Cambodia in the 1970s, when more than 1.5 million people were killed. The 1980s list of horrors includes Afghanistan, Angola, Ethiopia, and Sudan. The 1990s began with the struggles of the Kurds and went on to see the break up of Yugoslavia, with terrible suffering and death. There have also been the deaths and destruction in Chechnya, Sierra Leone and East Timor. At the time when 'Schindler's List' was attracting large audiences in Europe and America the shocking genocide was taking place in Rwanda. Today there is violent death, due to misunderstanding, hatred and fear, every day in the Middle East, and the people of the three faiths, Jews, Muslims and Christians, all children of Abraham, suffer terribly. As I write this epilogue war rages in Iraq with unknown consequences.

Our hope in publishing this book is that it will do much more than provide readers with knowledge about the holocaust. Our hope is that our book, like the old rug flapping in the breeze, may begin to offer an insight which will move readers on to making connections, to meeting people, and to bridge building and peace making in our dangerous and fragile world. Our hope is the same as the hope of the national holocaust day, "To ensure that the horrendous crimes, racism and victimisation committed during the holocaust are neither forgotten nor repeated, whether in Europe or elsewhere in the world."

Most of the lectures which are brought together here were given by people with a personal link to those who suffered in the Holocaust. Leah Dickstein for example began her talk on women survivors of the camps by describing some of the people she knew personally who had suffered. Joel Elkes, who gave the first lecture, is the son of Elchanan Elkes, a hero of the Kovno Ghetto and of Miriam Elkes, a concentration camp survivor. Joel and Sara Elkes initiated the lectures in honour of their parents and have encouraged the publication of this book. I am fortunate to know Sarah as a friend and to have met Joel. I have also met Ilana Ash and heard her tell the story with which we begin this collection, so it has been a little easier for me than for many others to move beyond knowledge of 'what was done' to commitment to awareness, bridge building and peace making.

I write as a Christian who thinks of Jesus as a great bridge-builder. He was the 'crucified Jew' whose death was followed by centuries of persecution for his people. Some writers have seen the Holocaust as a sign of the unity of the Christ with Judaism and with Christianity.

The Hebrew Bible and the New Testament are full of stories of bridge building. One of the stories in the Hebrew Bible is of Ruth. It is set in the time of the Judges but was written down after the Babylonian exile. Ruth was a Moabite woman who was married to an Israelite who had died. She unexpectedly stayed with Naomi, her mother-in-law, and has thus always been celebrated as a bridge builder between peoples, an example and a challenge to us all.

If we do feel the breeze when we read this book, if we are moved to become peace makers in our world, we will also realise that the barriers we set out to move are often invisible at first, beginning in a very small way and growing large not only through deliberate planning but also through accident, through myth, fear, prejudice and above all ignorance. There was anti-semitism throughout Europe between the two world wars, which grew gradually, sometimes, but not always, helped by discriminatory laws. In 1930s Germany there was a clear plan first of all, through the introduction of new laws, to make Jewish people second class citizens and then to annihilate them.

One of the main lessons of the history of the Holocaust, and of earlier and later atrocities, is that any 'civilisation' is fragile and that barbarism may break through at any time and become the norm. Those who ran the concentration camps were ordinary people, going home to their ordinary families. We are all ordinary people. We are all vulnerable and we are all fragile. Can we be sure that we would be heroes if we were faced with a choice of letting an evil comment or action pass us by or of standing out from the crowd and perhaps risking danger? Our work for peace, reconciliation and justice must begin with ourselves and we must be ever vigilant in every circle we move in. It is sometimes because we are careless in small matters that we become immobilised by fear when we are faced by bigger challenges.

We offer this book as a contribution to understanding between peoples and as an encouragement to the growth of courage and responsibility for bridge building in our one world. It is also a warning of what can happen when we fail to take up the challenge.

Contributors

Yehuda Bauer
Director of the International Institute for Holocaust Research,
Yad Vashem, Jerusalem.

Leah J Dickstein
Professor of Psychiatry and Behavioural Sciences, University of
Louisville, Kentucky.

Joel Elkes
University Distinguished Senior Professor Emeritus of Psychiatry,
Johns Hopkins University, Maryland.

Martin Gilbert
Honorary Fellow of Merton College, Oxford.

Deborah Lipstadt
Director of the Institute for Jewish Studies, Dorot Professor of Modern
Jewish and Holocaust Studies, Emory University, Atlanta, Georgia.

Michael Marrus
Professor of History, Dean of the School of Graduate Studies,
University of Toronto, Canada.

Aubrey Newman
Professor of History (Emeritus), Founding Director of the Stanley
Burton Centre for Holocaust Studies, University of Leicester.

Stephen Smith
Founding Director, Beth Shalmon Holocaust Centre, Laxton, Newark,
UK.